# Trump: America Loves A Winner

## Understanding the Trump Phenomenon

# By Ken Julien

**Published by Julien Media**
ISBN-13:978-1530345526  2016

Email: kj@getmesometrump.com
Blog: getmesometrump.com
Twitter: @getmesometrump

# Contents

# Introduction

I am closer to the end of my life than the beginning. This book is written with the hope that the same is not true of the American dream. Like a person, our country started its life full of dreams of what could and can be. And as we grew this country has become a more positive force for the advancement of mankind than any other in the history of mankind. We've made mistakes and we've achieved great accomplishments. We've had times of laughter and times of sorrow. We've experienced times of prosperity and times of hardship. Throughout it all we have never given up trying to be better, to do better. Sadly, we now seem to be losing our way. Not our people, but our system. Our system seems to be corrupted by a virus. A virus that attacks all that is good.

This presidential cycle is unlike any our country has ever witnessed. Candidates with names like Donald Trump appear to have become beacons of hope reaching out to guide our country back onto the path of greatness. The names don't seem as important as what they are saying. Their names could just have easily been Smith or Garcia. They are giving hope to the people that want to do better, to be better. They are standing up to the virus that has infected our system. They are showing people that all is not lost. That we can in fact be great again. Trump proposes taking us forward by taking us back to our roots.

This book is not about Donald Trump but yet it is. I've never read a book written by or about Trump. I've never even met the man. But I've listened to what he has said and witnessed the reaction to what he is saying. Many Americans are frustrated with our political leadership. They are mad as hell and he is saying what they are thinking. Many Americans feel powerless to stop the madness. I believe that Trump more than any other candidate has the formula to end the madness. Love him or hate him, Trump's message is resonating with millions of American people. The entrenched establishment is terrified of him. This became obvious to me months ago when he made his announcement that he was indeed running to become President of the United States. It was brash, unfiltered and completely politically incorrect. People loved it and the establishment lashed out at it.

I visited the BILL & MELINDA GATES foundation visitors center in Seattle recently. The foundation is perhaps the largest individual charitable effort ever undertaken. In bold capital letters it states - **EVERY PERSON DESERVES THE CHANCE TO LIVE A HEALTHY, PRODUCTIVE LIFE.** To me this phrase represents the basis of the American dream. It does not say, every American, it states every person. It says, the chance, it does not say the guarantee. For many years the American system has provided the people at home and many around the world the best opportunity for that chance.

The American system has now become so corrupted that it has turned on itself. It breeds division rather than brotherhood. It has strayed from its' past when citizens temporarily took time off from their professions to serve their country. Citizens that were farmers, ranchers, doctors, lawyers and a variety of other professions. Now we are being ruled, rather than served, by a class of permanent professional politicians. This has resulted in an extraordinary imbalance between the elites and the rest of us.

Suddenly Trump takes the stage and shakes things up. He is uniquely qualified to usher in a change due to his wealth, accomplishments and force of personality. He doesn't need fame, money or power. He already has them. He is running to make America great, not to make himself great. He is running for president as a citizen not as a professional politician. He is using his own money to campaign. If elected, he won't owe anything to anyone except the American people. Should he be successful, he may usher in a new era of true public servants rather than the professional politicians of today.

This book is intentionally short and simplistic. Sometimes the clearest and best solutions aren't complicated. I have tried to be kind although the truth is not always gentle. I have tried not to criticize individuals although some specific names were required for context. It may seem like a statement of the obvious to the die-hard Trump supporters. They sense that they like what is happening but may not be certain why. Hopefully it will allow them to better clarify why it is that they are moved by Donald Trump. To many people including the "establishment", younger people and others it is a puzzling phenomenon. I am writing this book to put into words the Trump phenomenon from the perspective of an ordinary coach-class American. Love him or hate him it is worth paying attention to Donald Trump because he has the potential to fundamentally change politics as we know it. For those of you trying to wrap your heads around what is happening here, read on!

# Swimming Against the Tide

"People need to believe they can make a
difference - that one person standing
strong can turn the tide."
Ann Aguirre

If you have ever sat on a beach you have
surely marveled at the relentless procession
of waves lapping at the sand. Minute after
minute, hour after hour, day after day, year
after year the waves relentlessly, endlessly,
keep rolling in. Picture in your mind a bottle
riding upon each of these waves. Inside each
bottle is an unpaid bill with your name on it.
You stuff these bills in your pockets. Then
you need more room so you stuff them in your
backpack. Then you need still more room so
your fill your cooler with bills. You still
run out of room but the never-ending waves
keep coming. You realize there is no way you
could ever pay all of these bills. You look
down the beach and everyone is collecting
their own bottles.

Eventually you need to rest while the
bottles pile up at your feet. You pick a bill
out of your pocket and examine it. Suddenly
you realize that you didn't buy this stuff.
When you look down the beach everyone is

yelling "hey I didn't buy this crap". You are becoming angry and confused so you look closer at a bill. You notice in the small print that it says that your parents or someone else signed your name for their purchase. Everyone is now screaming "my parents didn't get my permission to put me into endless debt"! An accountant on the beach has estimated the amount of all the bills scooped up by everyone so far to be almost $60,000 for every adult and child on the beach. And yet they keep coming. All you wanted was a nice picnic at the beach!

The bottles on the waves were imaginary, but the $60,000 in debt for every man, woman and child in American is real. Over $19 trillion in total as a country. Yet the bad news keeps coming. This amount is only for our federal debt, we haven't even taken into account state and local government debt. Just unpaid bills for state government employee pensions alone are estimated to come in at over $4,000 per person. And this amount doesn't count an estimated $80-$100 trillions of future bills for promises such as Social Security and Medicare. Isn't everyone sick and tired of adjusting their own purchases as things cost more and real wages decline? Then why do we allow the politicians to spend without limits?

So how did we get in this mess if we didn't personally sign for all these debts? We voted for them, that's how. Every time we voted for an elected official we either directly or indirectly authorized them to spend our tax money as they please and run up debts on our behalf. You could also have chosen not to vote and let other people select on your behalf. Those votes also allow elected officials to decide many other things for you. You authorized them to decide what freedoms you can keep. They decide if you can worship as you want, if you can have a gun, which doctor you can see, what you can say publicly, who can enter the country, if we should have safe streets, how you should be protected from terrorists and an endless list of other matters. Still think it doesn't matter which candidate you vote for?

There are estimated to be over 500,000 elected officials in this country. These officials manage millions of employees. All of these people are making decisions, small or large, on our behalf. I can hear it now; I didn't want them to have all this power. Not to worry, they have thousands of lobbyists to help them make the right choices for you. Unfortunately, not many of us has a lobbyist working on our behalf. There is also the Constitution of the United States to put a limit on what they can do. But popular culture is drifting toward an attitude of interpreting the Constitution as an old outdated piece of paper not to be taken too seriously.

The nine justices of the Supreme Court are the last barrier between your freedoms under the Constitution and the politicians' actions. Possibly the most important duty of a president, outside of war, is the nomination of Supreme Court Justices. Currently we have four justices that believe the constitution should be the ultimate authority in protecting our rights. We also have four justices that have demonstrated that they believe the

Constitution represents just a piece of paper containing suggestions that can be overridden by current social desires. And we have one justice who can't seem to make up his mind. We also have a president that feels he has the power to ignore the Constitution if it doesn't agree with him.

We are truly standing on the precipice. The next president will more than likely nominate at least one new justice. That justice may decide if we jump into the abyss of a Constitution-less country. That one justice could give the government the legal right to take all that you earn and ring up unlimited debt. They may decide you can no longer hang a Christian symbol on the front of your home or own a gun. It may sound far-fetched but it is happening in many areas of our life. It may also sound good if you want guns taken away. Consider that it could also happen to freedoms you cherish. If they can take away your guns, they can take away your Iphones. Wouldn't be as much fun then.

Let's be crystal clear about one thing. There is no happy ending to the debt story. The only ways out are rampant inflation or bankruptcy. Either choice would result in Americans living like the citizens of a third-world country. We are adding to our debt each and every day by spending more than we make. We are expanding our funding requirements every time someone crosses our borders and is provided a comfortable work-free life. We are adding to our debt spiral every time a politician gives out free anything with money we don't have to give. We are blissfully "getting ours" while we selfie our way to serfdom.

But there is hope that we can stem the tide of debt. As long as we maintain the strongest economy in the world we can support the debt we have. We just need to stop adding to it. Here is where a businessperson like Trump can help. He has spent his whole life operating under the principle that a business can't incur endless amounts of debt with no possible ability to repay them. We simply cannot continue to pile on the debt and expect that dire consequences will not follow. Calling people who tell the truth about our spending and debt negative and mean-spirited will not stem one wave of the tide. Trump is not afraid to tell the truth.

# Make America Great Again

"Mr. Gorbachev, tear down this wall!"
Ronald Reagan

To understand the Trump Phenomenon, you need to consider what Trump might mean by "Make America Great Again". I am old enough to remember when Ronald Reagan was elected President of the United States of America. Our country was the greatest country in the world but we were mired in gloom. We didn't act great, we didn't appear great and we certainly didn't feel great. American hostages were being held captive by Iran, jobs were scarce, inflation was rampant, oil was in short supply and the Soviets were rattling their nuclear weapons. Even so, we were great but didn't feel or act like it. Reagan's optimism, strength of character and talents put us back on the road to greatness. We felt united, not divided. Reagan's strength began the unraveling of the Soviet empire. He stood at the Berlin Wall and shouted at the Soviets – "tear down this wall". They did just that. The 52 American hostages held by Iran were released the day Reagan was inaugurated after 444 days of captivity. Our economy began to grow again.

Fast forward to today. America is still the greatest country on the planet. Unfortunately, we feel less great than we were or we could be. We feel the greatness slipping away. Donald Trump is a winner. He is a strong personality and he wants to make America great again. This has resonated with millions of American people. What might Trump mean by make American great again? And what are the world-wide implications?

No country in the history of the world has been "great" without a strong military and a strong economy. America has had both of these for over a century. Unfortunately, both are currently in decline. It is folly to believe lofty social goals can be achieved without either of these. In fact, without either of these we will be talking about how we can survive rather than how we can thrive.

History is replete with examples of great Western societies that resulted in human advancement. Examples range from Egypt 4,000 years ago to Babylon 3,000 years ago to Rome 2,000 years ago to the Incas 500 years ago to Great Britain in the last few centuries. They advanced science, communication, architecture, arts, medicine and many other disciplines. Unfortunately, they all had their flaws to varying degrees. All relied on military conquest. Most relied on slavery. They were all economic and military superpowers. They all eventually declined. As they declined their areas of influence fell into a dark period for a great many years. The one exception was Great Britain when America stepped into the void.

When Rome declined the consequences for the Western world were traumatic. Western society went into more than a 1,000-year state of chaos. Vicious bands of people ranged freely taking what they could through killing and plundering. Micro societies developed, banding together for protection. Advancement of science and the arts almost ceased. Large numbers of people died from starvation and disease. Human advancement came to a virtual standstill as survival became all consuming. The Pantheon, built by the Romans in 125 A.D., remained the largest concrete structure built in the world for over 1,000 years! Roads built by the Romans were still being used by people from England to the Middle East for over 1,000 years. The world without a great society was not a nice place.

Upon the founding of America, a new great country began to emerge at home and on the world stage. The Declaration of Independence and the Constitution dared the American people to dream of a better country than had ever existed. Many of those dreams were attained. They accomplished great things. They have contributed to the advancement of science, architecture, law and countless other disciplines. Although it took too long, the scourge of slavery was wiped from our shores by a civil war at the cost of hundreds of thousands of human lives that were given for the cause. They put a man on the moon. They created unprecedented individual liberties for American citizens including freedom of speech and religion. They created the most generous and charitable country ever to grace the earth. They fought and won world wars they neither started, nor wanted, to defeat the horrors of Nazi Germany and Imperial Japan. They completely defeated nations in war, helped them rebuild then left them to govern themselves. Has America been perfect? Of course not. The Vietnam war is an example of that. Generally, I think it is fair to say Americans have tried to do the right thing for the right reasons.

Unfortunately, it has become more popular to criticize our country than to contribute to it. We have become a nation of whinny spoiled children that throw a tantrum when we don't get everything we want. We have a President that apologizes for being American and actually bowed to the Saudi King. We have politicians that seek to fracture rather than unite us. We are losing hope, without which nothing good is possible. We have people who want to reduce civil liberties like religion, gun ownership and free speech. We have a movement to selectively enforce laws. An anger has built up that has propelled presidential candidates like Donald Trump and Bernie Sanders to the top of the early 2016 polls. Americans don't feel the greatness. Regardless of how disillusioned and mad people may be, we still have the strongest economy and military in the world.

Although our military is still the strongest in the world, just how strong it has been has varied over the past decades primarily due to economic reasons. Republicans have tended to build up our military. Democrats have tended to reduce our military, spending the money on social programs instead. We are currently embarked on an aggressive program of reducing military spending. If we ever reach the point where our military power is not at least the equal of any other nation it is game over. Financially our dollar would decline in value. It would buy less and our lifestyle would decline accordingly. The interest rate on our debt would soar. We would no longer be able to borrow unlimited amounts of money to fund our lifestyles. Many instances of nations suffering economically due to their currency declining have occurred during my lifetime.

Unfortunately, it seems to be in our human DNA to want what other people have. If we weren't strong militarily then other people would try to take what we have. An analogy from prior to the "polite" police at schools is illustrative. The bully would always spot the weak kid in the schoolyard and take something from them. If America was not strong we would be the weak kid. If our dollar was worthless we would not have lunch money to hand over in order to prevent a beating from the bully. And there would be no world "bully" cop to protect us. In essence we would have no way to protect our safety.

Our country is $19 trillion dollars in debt. The last two presidents have each incurred more debt than all the presidents preceding them combined. Bush doubled the existing debt when he was elected and then Obama doubled it again. Sounds like a Ponzi scheme to me. In addition, we have no plan that will allow us to pay for programs such as Social Security without borrowing the money. Trump is correct, it is a mess. We are blindly speeding down the road to ruin. No amount of denial will change the reality of the financial situation we are in.

If we continue down our current financial path it is a question of when, not if, our way of life will be over. There will be no goodies to be handed out by politicians. There will be no secure retirement. There will be nothing to hand down to our children except debt. We will not be safe in our own homes. We will spend our time talking about the good old days. Trump is a businessman. He understands the concept of matching your spending with your income. He understands that both financial and military strength are critical for our survival. He feels that he is the leader to provide the real world experience and strength to make America great again.

# Of Course Trump is Angry

"I'm as mad as hell, and I'm not going to take this anymore."
NETWORK

Of course Trump is angry, so are many Americans. Trump is saying that he is angry over what is happening to our country. Try to find someone who isn't. You can't turn on TV "news" or commentary programs without people shouting at one another. People are called racist, bigots, religious extremists, right wing or left wing simply because they have a different opinion. I guess it is easier just to insult people than to defend your opinion with facts. Even the President can't seem to make a public speech of any kind without looking angry and insulting people who disagree with him. Where is the laughter?

In 1976 a popular motion picture titled "Network" was released. The movie starred Peter Finch as a network anchor. He was the first actor to win a posthumous Academy Award for Best Actor in a leading role for his performance. In the film, Finch had a meltdown while live on air. Finch went into a tirade about the problems ordinary people faced and the hopelessness they felt in dealing with the problems. He then shouted the now memorable words "I'M AS MAD AS HELL, AND I'M NOT GOING TO TAKE THIS ANYMORE!". He then urged everyone watching his broadcast to get up and shout these words out their windows. They then cut to show people all around the country opening windows and shouting this phrase. Nothing explains the Trump phenomenon better than the scene from this film. Some of the issues have changed but most of them are the same. Finch shouted of crime, inflation, loss of or fear of losing a job, the environment and other current events. Consider that the film aired in 1977. That is almost 40 years ago and things have only gotten worse. No wonder people are mad.

The Republican elites dragged out South Carolina Republican Governor Nikki Haley to give the rebuttal to the 2016 Democrat State of the Union political address. She felt that we needed to ignore "the siren call of the angriest voices". The specific issue Ms. Haley brought up seemed to take issue with Trump's opposition to illegal immigration. She went on to say no one willing to work hard should feel unwelcome in this country. Many American are angry with the damage illegal immigration has done to our country. She is telling us that we have no right to be angry. Keep in mind that she was handpicked by Republican rulers to deliver this message. Her message was a thinly disguised attack on the Trump movement. Ok, so let's unpack this. This was not only an attack on Donald Trump but by association his supporters as well. Why would they attack their leading candidate in the Republican presidential primary and the millions of

Americans who support him? Could it be that they are scared of someone upsetting their applecart? It makes you wonder if they would rather lose the election than get bumped from their spot at the pork trough. After all the current elites are feeding pretty well at the public trough. Really Ms. Haley, are we supposed to sit down and shut up while the political elites run this country into the ground? Do the elites think we are stupid?

What are the things Trump is saying we are angry about? Often he frames things in terms of winning and losing. There is an old saying - if you are not winning then you are losing. If you are losing, you are feeling a loss of hope and a sense of powerlessness. Why are we feeling less hopeful and more powerless? It is because we are feeling that we have lost control of the events affecting our daily lives. It is no accident that Obama won the last two elections on the message of hope and change. We got the change but obviously we're not feeling the hope eight years later. In January of 2016 a single power ball lottery reached 1.5 billion dollars. The amount of tickets bought is a perfect visualization of our thirst(hope) for a better life.

In order to define a solution to a problem you would first need to define the problem. Trump has spent considerable time to define the problems. Trump can appear negative by constantly identifying the problems. Unfortunately, unless he does identify the problems he cannot effectively outline his solutions. A book, like a campaign should lay out the problems before the solutions. As I write out the problems it makes me want to jump out of the window rather than shout out of it. Anyway here goes.

First and foremost, our standard of living is declining. We are losing the financial battle in our daily lives. Wages are falling far short of the amount needed to live a decent life. Meanwhile our costs of living are skyrocketing. We see the people on Wall Street and in Washington D.C. living large while we are living small. Taxes are out of control. Everything including income taxes, property taxes, sales taxes, use fees and now even hundreds of health care taxes from Obamacare. Everything seems to cost more including rents, cars, food, and most of all health care. People feel that if they work hard and play by the rules that they are being screwed.

Most of the increase in the cost of living has been loaded on us by the government and Wall Street. The government imposes thousands of regulations and taxes on our economy that end up costing us more. Health care is a perfect example. Insurance premiums and deductibles have skyrocketed as a direct result of Obamacare. Wall Street and the Federal Reserve create asset bubbles designed to enrich themselves at our expense. Interest rates have been driven to zero by the Federal Reserve. With zero interest rates, seniors cannot earn enough interest to support themselves. Rental housing is another example. Rents have been steadily increasing to the point of not being affordable for many Americans. Great for the landlords, not so much for the renters.

Trump hits hard on what are called "Free Trade" agreements signed by our professional politicians. Americans look around and see shuttered factories. They don't see living wage jobs. Fair Trade is code for the Clinton-Bush policy of cheap labor for business. They have entered into trade agreements that Trump feels have transferred millions of good jobs to other countries. Obama and Mrs. Clinton are now jumping on the free-trade train with their Trans-Pacific Partnership(TPP) that will kill more of our jobs. Both parties receive untold millions of political campaign dollars from big businesses that employ thousands of lobbyists. Understandably their lobbyists do not seem to have jobs, except theirs, as a high priority. I don't know about you but I don't employ a lobbyist. Our politicians pay attention to what their donors' lobbyists tell them. Therefore, as Trump says, we lose in all these agreements. He wants to win and as a result create jobs for you and I.

Trump spends a lot of time talking about our veterans. They have been under served by our government run health care system established for them. Thousands and thousands of them are homeless. You cannot drive in our cities without seeing the scores of homeless, many of whom are veterans. It has been estimated that 22 veterans commit suicide every day. Our government choses to spend our money in other ways. For instance, on people who enter the country illegally. We provide health care, feed, house and educate everyone who chooses to enter our country illegally. Even more appalling our President is bringing in thousands of "refugees", that may include terrorists, with the same fully paid great lifestyle. Yet our veterans, who make this country free, go without adequate health care and in many cases without a place to live. Trump is angry about this treatment of our veterans.

Americans are fearful about terrorism. They should be. We have had dozens and dozens of attacks in our country since 9/11. Most were not identified as terrorism by our government. Events such as shootings of police officers, be-headings in the Midwest, a shooting at Fort Hood, a bombing at the Boston Marathon, stabbings at a community college, most covered up as non-terrorist acts such as workplace violence or the work of unaligned "lone-wolves". Try as they may the government cannot hide the scourge of Radical Islamic Terrorism that has descended upon our land. Trump has proposed steps to prevent terrorism yet our government seems to choose political correctness over our safety. Trump has spoken out as being for our safety first.

Virtually every week a police officer is murdered on our streets. Is it just me or does it seem as if criminals are more valued than our police officers? We seem to treat criminals as heroes and police officers as the enemy. Some would go so far as to claim that the current administration has unleashed an unspoken war on the police. Reports of officers cutting back routine police work are rampant. Murder rates in the cities are skyrocketing. Even the home town of our president, Chicago, has seen murders skyrocket since the administration has started their "war" against law enforcement. Trump has expressed support for law enforcement.

There seems to be an almost unlimited number of ways politicians have devised to divide us. Rich-poor, black-white, straight-gay, advantaged-disadvantaged, male-female, Republican-Democrat and on and on. Many Americans are tired of politicians and media elites that seek to divide us for their own purposes. For professional politicians there is much to be gained by division - votes and contributions.

Probably the biggest disappointment of the Obama reign is the deterioration of race relations. There was a lot of hope that Obama would bring us together rather than seek to tear us apart. He chooses to spend more time with Hollywood celebrities than he does in the inner cities. There is anger on the streets as can be seen virtually every night on the news. Of course people are marching, they see failing schools, no jobs, crime in their neighborhoods and feel alienated from the police. Hell yea they are mad, can you blame them. You see it, I see it and certainly Trump sees it. As Americans we see scenes of marches on the streets way too often. Yes, we are mad about it. Whether marching or watching you would have to be one sick puppy to smile about what is happening. Trump doesn't talk much about differences. He seems to view people as Americans. Rather than seek to divide us he speaks of us as Americans. He doesn't dwell on our differences.

We see the politicians encouraging illegal immigration that further divides us. An effort is being made by politicians to discourage assimilation by new immigrants. The costs of this policy increases our debt and makes it harder for us to find jobs. Trump does not support illegal immigration. Trump doesn't need to stoke division among us to get donations because he is paying for his own campaign. It is refreshing to see a candidate that doesn't seek to categorize and divide us.

People see their country being run by and for the establishment elites and special interests. They are angry about this. Internally generated anger by millions of Americans is nothing new. During the Vietnam War we were angry and took to the streets. We were protesting the establishment's war. In those days we referred to the establishment as "the man". Well, people got mad enough and "the man" ended the war. Trump is counting on enough people being angry to make big changes in professional politics and our country. Trump seems to be channeling peoples' anger into voter action. His rallies are being attended by throngs of people. The anger is real. Trump's hope is that people will vote for him as an alternative to the corrupt divide and conquer professional politicians.

# The Media Elites

"Get your facts first, then you can
distort them as you please."
Mark Twain


Make no mistake the media elites are not
your best friends. They make millions of
dollars, they get their hair and make-up
fussed over every day by the "little" people,
they get chauffeured to and fro, they live in
secluded enclaves, they socialize with the 1%
and their children attend private schools. You
don't sit next to them at soccer games, you
don't tailgate with them at football games,
you don't wait with them in a crowded doctor's
waiting room and you certainly don't bump into
them at Walmart or Safeway. Does that make
them bad people? Of course not. It is just
that they don't live like you. As Bill Clinton
might say - they don't feel your pain. How
could they? Everything was coming up roses for
these elites until Trump crashed their party.

No matter if he wins the election or goes
down in flames, Trump has changed main stream
media as we know it. Is it any wonder that the
biggest applause moments at his rallies occur
after he attacks the media? Trump pulled back
the curtain on the media like Dorothy's dog

Toto did to the Wizard of Oz. When Toto pulled back the curtain it revealed an old gasbag speaking into a microphone, not the infallible Wizard that everyone assumed was there.

No single moment illustrates the Trump effect on the media than the first Fox News Republican debate. The Fox Queen, Megyn Kelly, launched into a vicious attack on Trump in her first tirade posed as a question about his attitude toward women. I suspect that she thought he would cower in her presence and defer to her brilliance. He did not. Trump fought back and exposed her bias against a non-establishment candidate. The game was on! This struck a chord with many people watching the debate. This was what they were waiting for, a person who would not be bullied into looking like the person someone in media tried to paint them as being. Viewers had seen that movie way too many times.

In 2012 CNN's Candy Crowley, posing as a non-biased moderator injected herself into the presidential debate by blatantly taking Obama's side over Romney's. It was particularly evident during a discussion on Benghazi when she defended Obama's truthfulness. Romney did not aggressively stand up for himself. He allowed himself to be bullied. He looked weak. He lost the election. Is there any wonder why people cheered Trump as he took on the Fox team as they tried to weaken his candidacy? The American people don't want a pansy as the leader of the free world. If you can be bullied by "talking heads" how could you possibly defeat ISIS?

Main stream media has historically been

the domain of TV, radio and large circulation print such as magazines and newspapers. Although their influence has diminished due to the internet it is nonetheless very influential. It is often referred to as "the media". Historically the media attempted to present an independent view of events that were unfolding around us. It has morphed into more of an advocacy tool to present the particular opinion of those who control the particular media source. The media has been under an assault upon their dominance influence over the publics' view of world events. The internet and alternative media sources have increasingly been attracting peoples' time and attention for years.

The injection of opinion into "news" has turned off many people. The talking heads constantly shouting and interrupting each other has become annoying. They constantly try to tear large groups of us down and divide us. They look unhappy and they sound unhappy. Sometimes while watching them I think I've dozed off and mistakenly turned on the Jerry Springer show. Americans don't like unhappy. Americans like laughter. These media trends have resulted in two significant challenges for the media. Profitability for the media owners has been declining and their influence over the American people is in a state of decline. In plain English they are losing power and money, the opiate of the elites.

Trump has been on TV almost day and night. Interestingly he has been on CNN on a regular basis. Why is that? CNN has been a staunch supporter of Democrat candidates for years. It is hard to say. There could be many reasons but none more obvious than an increased number of viewers. Or it could be something as devious as thinking he could be easier to beat than a Republican establishment candidate. Who cares? The point is that Trump is changing media dynamics by the force of his personality. It seems everyone wants to interview "The Donald". That certainly seems like a good thing. Give the people what they want instead of what you want to give them. Let the voters decide where to go from there. Adapt or die is a fundamental law of nature.

Fox has so far resisted the new reality. With some exceptions, they continue to support any establishment candidate in an effort to defeat Trump. They continue to state all the reasons Trump can't win. Keep in mind that political candidates spend billions of dollars on advertising. The media rely on these ads for profits. Trump is not spending large amounts of money on ads. It would be normal for the media to dislike the lack of ad spending. Trump is getting visibility without the ad spending. He is attracting five, ten and fifteen thousand people to his rallies. He is being shown on TV because people want to hear what he has to say therefore they will watch a program just because he is covered. He is attacking the media because of the way they have acted. It would be normal for the media to be frightened by this type of candidate.

I can't watch or read everything the media produces. From my limited perspective the biggest change I've noticed since Trump entered the race has been at CNN. Nothing has been more striking to me than the town hall gun control forum with Obama that was aired by

CNN and moderated by Anderson Cooper. It was a balanced and civil discussion, even with a highly opinionated President. Honestly I never thought I would see the day when CNN would present both sides to an issue with a President they strongly supported being so vocally on one side of the issue. Was this because of the Trump effect on the media? We'll never know.

Trump has unquestionably had an impact on the media. No single event illustrates this point more than the removal of the Union Leader newspaper from the Republican debate in New Hampshire. The Union Leader is the largest newspaper in New Hampshire. They published a front page editorial insulting Trump. Trump then insisted they be removed from the "neutral" debate. They were in fact removed by ABC. This may have been an unprecedented display of courage and strength of character by a candidate. Instead of begging for forgiveness he stood his ground and said what needed to have been said for years to the media. Simply, that a clearly biased organization had no business being involved in the electoral debate process. The debate forum is designed to provide the voting public with an opportunity to make decisions regarding the candidates. It is not intended to provide a venue for the media to express their biased opinions.

Not all of the media run in the same herd. Some individuals have built their own brand to a point that they can say, without fear, what they feel is the truth. And quite frankly some see things as they really are more clearly than others. I hesitate to say this for fear of being called a "ditto head" but Rush Limbaugh is an example. Some others include Sean Hannity, Bill O'Reilly, Mike Broomhead, Mike Gallagher, Joe Scarborough, Laura Ingraham and Chris Cuomo. They say what they think without fear of recrimination because they are their own brand. Not unlike Trump, no one is the boss of them. Limbaugh has, as Trump would say, a "huge" audience. ABC, NBC, and CBS used to control the "news" airwaves but have now become almost irrelevant. The American public has simply changed the channel after too many years of their biased "news" reporting. Will they adapt? We will see.

This chapter is near the front of the book for a reason. Before we can understand the Trump Phenomenon we have to wipe our slate clean of what we are told to believe by the media. They are powerful enablers of the current political system. They benefit from leaving things the way they are. By the time you read this book much may have changed. Sanders and or Trump may be on the way to victory in the election. If that is the case the media establishment elites will be jumping on the alternative candidate train with both feet. If they don't, they risk losing their influence, power and money.

# Americans, not Republicans or Democrats

"The men who crave power are best fitted
to acquire it and least-fitted to exercise it"
Exodus: God and Kings

I suspect Trump would have run as a third
party candidate if he thought he could be
elected in that manner. More and more people
are choosing to identify themselves as
Independent. They are sick and tired of being
categorized as being mindless followers of the
political class elites. The elites of both
parties revel in calling themselves "public
servants". I want to throw up when I hear
about the professional politicians' "lifetime
of public service". The top elites of them
have lived in unimaginable luxury on our tax
dollars and personally made millions of
dollars from political connections. One
current "royal" family of politicians has made
over $100 million dollars from their "lifetime
of public service". And they are not alone.
Meanwhile the standard of living for Americans
is steadily declining. Exactly what service
have they rendered to us? Maybe that is why
Americans have been drawn to candidates like
Trump, Sanders and other "outsiders". Can we

just stop calling all career politicians public servants!

    Donald Trump has shouted to the American people - you don't need a political class to rule over you! Many people are sick and tired of the Bushes and Clintons acting as if they are entitled to be president. Americans fought a revolution to throw off the yoke of rule by the King of England. Many would now claim we are being ruled by a faux royalty in the form of professional politicians. As the old saying goes - if you treat them like royalty they will treat you like subjects. Many Americans are revolting against this rule and they see Trump leading the revolt. What he has done is like someone throwing a fire bomb into the center of a medieval royal court. No wonder the professional politicians are scared.

    Professional politicians of both parties are more alike than they are different. They seek to categorize and divide us in search of votes and money. They have redefined the phase - go along to get along. They changed it to - go along to get mine. They craft carefully worded speeches specifically written for a particular audience. They then read these speeches off of a Teleprompter. Why do they do this? Could they be afraid that they may actually say what they believe if they spoke spontaneously? They seek to carefully control their responses to questions. Hillary Clinton has actually gone so far as to rope off reporters during one of her meet the people walks. The elites of the Democratic National Committee(DNC) have scheduled the Democrat primary debates at times obviously designed to attract as few viewers as possible. Republican debates, with Trump center stage, are scheduled to attract as many viewers as possible. You can judge who wants people to hear what they have to say.

Trump speaks extemporaneously. He doesn't need speech writers or Teleprompters to tell him what to say. He wants you hear what he thinks and believes. You may not like everything he says but at least you know what he is thinking. He says things that may seem outrageous and extreme. I believe he often speaks in extremes in order to get attention. In a sense he is going big rather than going home. He is opening a dialog on many issues that we have been afraid to discuss for fear of being labeled as evil human beings. The truth of what he believes hits you in the face like a tossed glass of cold water. Galileo said " All truths are easy to understand once they are discovered; the point is to discover them." With most politicians one would need to be a mind-reader to discover the truth of their beliefs. Do we really want to be ruled by politicians who hide their true beliefs for fear that we might discover them?

Jeb Bush has said that Donald Trump is not a Republican. In many ways he is right. Donald Trump is an American first as most of us are. I expect a HUGE number of Democrats to vote for Trump in a general election because they also view themselves as Americans first. Over 40% of Americans identify themselves as Independents. For most of our history America has been ruled by two political parties. One identified by a donkey, the other by an elephant. That just about sums it all up! More Americans are deciding they want out of the zoo.

Both parties have very passionate core members. Republicans and Democrats are faced with the challenge of keeping a large enough core of voters to win elections. It is hard to describe them without generalizing so please bear with me. Democrats have a propensity to accomplish this by handing out goodies like food stamps, disability benefits, free anything and everything. They have a very large core of voters who want no part of being "Independent" of these goodies. Democrats tend to vote 100% in line with their Party on issues. Republicans have historically been non-Democrats. Their herd is more fractured. As an example, in the 2016 Presidential primary the Republicans had over a dozen candidates compared to just three for the Democrats. Republicans have tended to give the goodies to businesses, but count on love of our country, religion or a strong military for many of their votes. Republican Senators Rand Paul and Ted Cruz are examples of Republican politicians who are not afraid to speak and vote against the positions of their party elites. As a result, they are taking their share of attacks by the Republican Establishment.

Trump is attempting to win the election by separating the less hard-core voters of both parties from their herd. He has chosen to run as a Republican. It was a smart decision. In 1992 a candidate similar to Donald Trump ran for President as an Independent. His name was Ross Perot and he was a successful businessman and he was wealthy. Like Trump, his campaign was largely self-funded. Many, but not all, of his positions were similar to Trump's. He lost. Perot did get 18% of the popular vote, the most by a third-party candidate since Theodore Roosevelt in 1912. It is generally thought that Perot took more of these votes from the Republicans. Bill Clinton was elected President over challenger George H.W. Bush. Many Republicans blamed Perot for their loss in the election. Trump may be a lot of things but he is no fool. He knew his history and saw that winning the Presidency as a third-party candidate was an uphill battle even if you were rich.

Trump had another reason to run as a Republican. He surely analyzed the base constituencies of each party. The Democrat Party views itself as the party of the little guy. That may be but they are also known as the party of handouts. My purpose is not to judge their motives but simply to put context to their base voting patterns. In any case, a large number of people who vote Democrat would not vote any other way. Many are living well without working and are not about to take the Food Stamps out of their own mouths. Who can blame them. Why would they vote for Trump? If I was making a good living off the government I wouldn't vote for him either. To give you an idea about how many people we are talking about consider that over 45,000,000 people are receiving food stamp benefits alone. That is an increase of approximately 17,000,000 people since Obama took office eight years ago as the American "safety net" morphed into a lifestyle. Draw your own conclusions.

Trump's choice to run as a Republican created obvious angst within the establishment elites of the Republican Party. The "elites" include a vast number of people and professions. They include vested elected officials such as the senior members of Congress. These senior elected officials have tremendous power to control their members. They hand out committee positions and raise contributions for less senior members. They base their hand-outs on loyalty(voting) for their positions. The Republican National Committee(RNC) bigwigs are part of this group. They enjoy enormous influence, financial rewards and power as a result of their employment. Campaign consultants and strategists, such as Karl Rove, are also included in this group. They also enjoy the same benefits. Lobbyists for Republican issues depend on bending the elites' ears for their livelihood. So as you can clearly see there is a lot at stake in maintaining the status quo.

Why are the elites so worried about Trump in particular? Quite simply, Trump is self-funding his campaign therefore he does not need the Party's money to run his election. If he does not need their money, he does not need to follow their advice. If he does not follow their advice, who needs them (the elites)? Certainly not the major donors who make large donations or pay the elites' generous salaries. Unsurprisingly the party elites waged an all-out war on his candidacy. They are raising millions of dollars through Political Action Committees(PACs). They are rallying their friends at Fox News and other sympathetic media outlets.

The first line of attack on Trump was - Trump can never win. This phrase became almost a mantra by the Republican elites. They followed a tried and true strategy of saying something over and over hoping people would eventually believe it to be true. I googled "trump cannot win" and it showed 161,000,000 results. There is no question they got their message out. It failed. Trump turned out to be a different breed of cat. He doesn't back down. He gave interviews to almost anyone. The media wanted the interviews because they knew ratings would go up if Trump was involved. People got to hear Trump's message directly from his mouth. His popularity increased. There are still the few die-hards chanting the mantra that he cannot win but they are starting to look foolish.

So the elites tried other strategies to get rid of Trump. One of my favorites is - wait until the "grown-ups" get interested. As if all Trump supporters are children. Give me a break. Didn't work. How about - Trump has no experience. Nope, supporters are not buying it. They realize that the politicians with experience got us in this mess to begin with. Then they moved on to - Trump has a passionate base but it is small, his negatives are too high, he started fast but he has plateaued and he is not conservative enough. Sorry but these attacks didn't work. They drag out intellectuals like George Will who questions Trump's intelligence, then collects his check and goes home. Not so fast Georgie boy. Trump hits back. Harder than ever. Trump questions Will's intelligence right back. Trump does not act like a wounded animal that slinks off into the night at the slightest sign of danger. I'm sure many media pundits are absolutely dumbfounded by Donald Trump. They simply seem incapable of understanding that people are fed up with politics as usual.

Then there are the debates. What a great venue to cut The Donald down to size. The first Fox News debate was a doozy. The establishment send out their crack team, led by Megyn Kelly, to put an end to this Trump nonsense. They angrily peppered him with questions designed to make him look bad. Ms. Kelly even stooped so low as to play the "Woman Card" on Trump. They stayed as far away as possible from the issues that voters care about. They relentlessly favored establishment candidates such as Bush. They did all they could to take him down but alas it was not enough. Trump came out stronger than ever and Fox News came out looking like an establishment tool. They tried to take Trump down again during the CNBC debates. Again the result was a disaster for the establishment. Then CNN schooled the other networks by doing a truly masterful job at presenting a debate about the candidates and their positions. The establishment had been routed.

The elites also evaluated getting rid of Trump by freezing him out of the technical aspects of the election process. They evaluated ways to keep him off primary ballots and talked of a brokered convention. Trump then told them flat out that if they don't treat him fairly he might run as an Independent. The elites knew this course of action would be a disaster for them, therefore they backed off of this course of action for now. Only a self-funding candidate like Trump could have won this skirmish. Time to move onto pro-establishment candidate ads funded by special interests' PACs. We will see how effective these are at the ballot box. You can see the ads running constantly on Fox News if you like. Make no mistake, the establishment will leave no tool in the toolbox to defeat an outsider like Trump. They may even try to "fix" the Republican convention if Trump arrives with a majority of votes but not enough to get the nomination.

This not only a Republican issue. Democrat candidate Bernie Sanders has also branded himself as an outsider. My guess is that he would also run independent of that party if he thought he could win in that manner. Trump has often reminded people that it is the Democrat Party not the Democratic Party as the media likes to refer to them. His message is that the people of the Democrat party are not represented equally. Democrats who are not affiliated with a special interest group such as unions or "disadvantaged" groups have not been equally served by the Democrat establishment. If you are not attached to a special interest group but just a hard working Democrat, you have been left behind. No wonder Sanders is attracting enormous support much to the surprise of the establishment. The establishment's "anointed" candidate, Hillary Clinton, has struggled to gain her rightful nomination. Many Democrat voters don't feel better off after years of rule by their party. The more they hear about the millions of dollars the Clintons have gotten from Wall Street the less they like it. Sanders is awakening the Democrat base to the duplicity of establishment candidates.

The bottom line is simply that Democrats

and Republicans alike, along with Independents, are sick and tired of the corruption that permeates our political system. In fact, only about 55% of the voting age population actually voted in the last presidential election. These non-voters have been called the "lost voters". These lost voters may be part of what Trump calls his "noisy majority". No doubt many of these lost voters were so disgusted with the system that they didn't think it mattered if they voted or not. Candidates like Trump, Carson and Sanders could change that. Although Sanders is hardly a non-politician he is being portrayed as one. In fact, there is polling by Reuters that suggest as many as one in ten people who cast a vote this year for president will do so for the first time in years or for the first time ever.

Record numbers of voters turned out the first time Obama was elected. If you recall, a big part of his pitch was "hope and change". The number of voters declined for his reelection. Guess people just didn't feel the hope four years after electing just another professional politician.

I have no doubt most politicians are good people and have good intentions. I also believe most ladies of the night are good people as well. But they both do what they do to get what they need or want. As Ronald Reagan once said "It has been said that politics is the second oldest professions, I have learned that it bears a striking resemblance to the first". There is no better way to describe our political system than corrupt. Politicians need money and votes to

survive. To get the money they must favor
their donors. Trump doesn't need their money;
he has his own. He doesn't need to be
dishonest to acquire fame, power and money. He
already has them. He is uniquely positioned to
break the bonds of corruption that bind our
political system. Trump will be free to do
what is best for all Americans. The
establishment can mock him, they can insult
him, they can misrepresent him, they can do
everything but control him.

# America's "Special Interests" Brand of Inequality

"When I have to choose between voting for the people or the special interests, I always stick with the special interests. They remember. The people forget."

Henry F. Ashurst

Does your government make you feel special? Didn't think so. Donald Trump feels he does not need to take one dollar from anyone to be elected President. Therefore, he doesn't owe anything to anyone except the people of this country for the privilege of serving as their president. That is a really easy concept for voters to understand. It is also a very appealing concept to voters. The slang in America is rife with implicit and explicit references to this concept. Just a few are: don't bite the hand that feeds you, got your six, you scratch my back and I'll scratch yours and quid pro quo. All meaning you do something for me and I expect to do something for you. My favorite is the Detroit City Councilwoman who shouted "bring home the bacon" as she explained how Obama owed them because they voted for him. Can you see anything wrong with this concept? Of course not.

Trump can and does say whatever he wants because he can. He is financially independent and emotionally secure. He does not need their money to get elected. He quite frankly doesn't appear to care what someone thinks about him. This is radically different than recent candidates for president. They pander for votes changing what they say from speech to speech, depending on the audience, because they need their votes. They vote for positions backed by their special interest donors because they need their money. Trump is ushering in a seminal change in political campaigning and it has the "establishment" terrified.

"Special Interests" are nothing more than people or organizations that have their own interests as their primary concern. It is arguably legal, certainly expected and almost encouraged by our current political system to bestow favors for votes and contributions. There doesn't seem to be anything wrong with that as long as you are not causing any harm. Ah but there's the rub. Our political system has become so corrupted that a special interest's gain almost always becomes someone else's loss. We seem to have lost the balance that our elected officials have been hired to maintain. That is heart of the corruption problem. Some politicians lose sight of the harm caused by the favors they bestow upon special interests. They do not strike a balance between the negative impacts on the people they were elected to represent with the positive impact to the special interest.

Although it may seem each special interest group is favored by one party or the other, that is not necessarily true. Wall Street is a perfect example. Most people probably believe the Republicans are the preferred party of Wall Street. That is not true. Recently they have given more donations to the Democrats. It's all about gaining influence wherever it resides. For many, but not all special interest groups, it means supporting both parties. Suffice it to say, politicians are all feeding at the special interest donation trough.

Alternative energy is all the craze lately. Understandably it is the current gold standard for special interest groups. There is more pork to be had than on all the pig farms in America. And more votes to be obtained than at an open bar, free chicken dinner at a political rally. It is large, technologically complex and confusing. Many people, myself included, care passionately about it. And it may or may not be critical to our future. For those of you who believe the science is settled on global warming, chill-out. Special interest groups can be deceptive sometimes. During the 1970s we were scared of global cooling. We were actually hard at work designing ways to make the earth warmer.

The alternative energy special interest group includes environmentalists, academicians, oil companies, railroads, pipelines, automobile companies and a list too long to detail. Technologies and energy sources involved range from hydrocarbons to solar to wind to electric cars and a multitude of others. The case of Tesla is a perfect case in point. Tesla makes electric cars for people that can afford to pay $100,000+ for a car. The founder of the company is now a billionaire donor. The people of America have paid for all this by governmental grants, tax credits and the like. In summary we turned a donor into a billionaire and subsidized expensive cars. We are further in debt while Tesla burns through our cash. And by the way those cars plug into our carbon energy based electrical system to recharge. Several more paragraphs will only cover the tip of the iceberg (pun intended).

As we discuss alternative energy it is important to remember we have an alternative right under our feet. The U.S. has more natural gas than any country on earth. Natural gas vehicle technology could be implemented quickly and it would create American jobs. It is a really cheap fuel source, many times cleaner than oil and could produce significant American jobs. In fact, a nighttime satellite image of gas-producing areas of our country reflects bright images of natural gas being burned off unused at the wellheads. So why don't we choose to save money, have a cleaner environment right now and create American jobs? Why wouldn't "environmentalists" rather have gas, that is being burned unused, utilized instead of dirtier oil as a fuel source. You guessed it, there are more political donations and votes to be had if we don't. The thinking seems to be that if we could solve the perceived problem that easily, a lot of government dollars would not be available to special interest donors with alternative solutions.

Let's take the issue of Iowa and ethanol since it plays such a big part in our political process. Winning the Iowa presidential primary is critical to the multitude of politicians who dream of becoming president. Ethanol is a fuel additive that can be made from corn, quite a bit of which is grown in Iowa. It is important to the farming lobbyists. Seems like a worthwhile environmental cause if it makes the environment cleaner and reduces the amount of oil used notwithstanding that it costs us more. Unfortunately, things are not as clear as they may seem. The production and transportation of ethanol uses approximately the same amount of fossil fuels as it saves at the gas pump. So no benefit there. The production of ethanol uses tremendous amounts of scarce water. Ethanol production also does considerable damage to the environment due to the large amounts of fertilizers used to grow the corn. The Mississippi river delta used to be the richest marine life area of our continental coastline. It is now a dead zone. It has been polluted primarily by the fertilizer residue flowing down the Mississippi river from the crop growing states. Not very friendly to the environment. The cost of food for Americans has increased as we use corn for fuel rather than food.

How about solar power and electric cars? They are both highly inefficient sources of energy. Why do we pay tens of thousands of taxpayer dollars for every Tesla electric car bought by taxpayers? Why do we generously subsidize solar panels made in China? These are hugely unprofitable enterprises run by large political donors. The founders and owners of these enterprises have made billion dollar personal fortunes driven by the various governmental subsidies. Meanwhile, your taxes, our national debt and costs of using energy have risen. Just saying.

We would rather transport oil in ships, subject to spills, from far away countries, some of whom support terrorism, than use our domestic sources. It seems that we oppose cheap domestic sources just to keep the money flowing to special interests; the big oil companies that have interests in foreign oil production and the multitude of alternative energy special interests. Rather than use more pipelines, we transport oil and natural gas by railroads, powered by hydrocarbons, that often experience spills causing damage to our environment. Opposition to the Keystone pipeline is a high profile example. Even the government concedes it would be a better environmental alternative than railroads. Turns out that a billionaire railroad owner is a large contributor and supporter of influential politicians.

As a country we have gone down a path of treating American oil, natural gas and coal as an inherently evil source of energy. This has happened even as technology has made the production, transportation and use of hydrocarbons safer, cheaper and more environmentally clean. We have blindly gone full steam into alternative energy without consideration of the consequences to all aspects of the environment or the tremendous cost to the public. In many cases we seem to be doing the wrong thing for what the public has been led(told) to believe is the right reason.

The pharmaceutical industry is a particularly glaring example of a special interest group. No one would argue that the development of new, safer and more effective medicines is not a worthwhile cause. But many Americans would argue that it is not fair that Americans pay 2 times, 4 times, 10 times or more for the same prescriptions than everyone else in the world. Why is that? Because our politicians mandate that it happen due the influence the industry exerts over them. We actually have laws that prohibit our government from negotiating lower drug prices for drugs paid for by the taxpayers. Other countries have laws prohibiting the drug companies from charging over a certain amount. In short, we pay higher prices and the rest of the world pays lower prices. Trump has said he would negotiate lower prices for us.

Even more egregious, U.S. based pharmaceutical companies are moving their headquarters and jobs overseas in order to pay less in taxes to the U.S. These moves contribute to a sky rocketing national deficit, lost jobs and millions of elderly Americans plunged into poverty as a result of mandated high prescription drug costs. Recently they have also exerted their influence to allow 11-year-old children to receive opiate based prescriptions, the gateway to heroin addiction.

No matter where you stand on Obamacare some things are crystal clear. Medical costs for Americans are soaring. Insurance premiums and deductibles are increasing dramatically. Insurance company profits are at record highs. Special interest groups at work once again. Many of the thousands of Obamacare regulations were designed and drafted by the special interest lobbyists. Corrupt politics at its finest! Special interests get what they want and politicians get what they want. Win-win. But what about the people who pay the bills? Guess we should have hired a lobbyist.

Let's talk briefly about education. The teachers' and administrators' union bosses are very influential people in our electoral process. They control vast sums of union dues from their members. They also have influence over their members' opinions. They are the Goliath of the special interests in the gigantic education system. Through donations and thought influence(votes) for their preferred politicians they have helped shape our existing educational system. As a result, our nation spends significantly more to educate a student than any other nation in the world. Yet our student performance lags sorely behind many other countries. I find it hard to believe that our teachers are not just as talented as any in the world. They just need to be allowed to do their job.

Burdensome governmental regulations are a primary reason education costs have been driven up to unconscionable levels. Politicians have learned that the best way to influence people is to control what they are taught. They do this by regulating what is acceptable and what is not. This practice is nothing new, totalitarian regimes have used this tactic throughout history. Universities support the politicians that benefit them. A case in point is a $300,000 speaking fee paid by UCLA to a current presidential candidate. That money could have better used to reduce the cost of education for all students.

Many special interests have a hand in this problem. They range from student loan lenders to university administrators. There is virtually no one speaking out for the families and students that have to pay or borrow for a college education. Many students are saddled with student loans that they may never be able to pay off. Many are precluded from buying a house due to the student loans hanging over their heads. I recently paid $450 just for a parking pass for my son to attend a university. That is almost as much as I paid for a full year of tuition when I was in school! This is what happens when virtually all the special interests are lined up on the side of spending. Students and families lack a strong advocate for their needs that include reducing the costs.

These are but a few examples of special interest groups at work. There are literally thousands more but you get the idea. There are as many on the "left" as there are on the "right". The financial cartel, covered in the next chapter, is by far the largest. None of these groups necessarily have bad intentions. They are simply playing the hand that was dealt to them. They could just as easily work more for the benefit of the American people if that was the way the game(system) was designed. Even within our system they manage to make great contributions to mankind.

Let's be clear, Trump has legally donated large sums of money to obtain political influence. Trump is a very successful international businessman. He couldn't thrive in our system of free enterprise if he didn't play the game the way it is designed. It would be similar to fighting with one arm tied behind your back. Trump has donated money to politicians of both parties. He has even donated money to the Clintons. Get over it. It does not mean that he agrees with all their political views.

Donald Trump, if elected President, would start from a position of not owing any special interest favors to anyone for their contributions. He is also a master negotiator. He even wrote a bestselling book "The Art of the Deal". His business accomplishments speak to his ability to bring parties with different interests together and reach a mutually favorable outcome. No one could build skyscrapers though out the world if they could not. Professional politicians simply cannot do this because of their need to favor special interests in order to be elected. No wonder many people feel that Trump is the answer to ending the special interests' domination of their daily lives.

# The Wall Street/Washington Cartel of Mass Destruction

"I believe that banking institutions are more dangerous to our liberties than standing armies."
Thomas Jefferson

The Wall Street-Washington cartel is the mother of all special interest groups. It is also unique in that the professional politicians can double dip into the money pot. First, they receive large donations from Wall Street while in office or while seeking office. Then they can work for, or get paid for giving speeches to Wall Street firms when they leave office. Nice gig if you can get it. Were I to write a screenplay about the Wall Street-Washington cartel it would be a gangster movie. Unfortunately, it would contain no drama since all their activities are carried out in the open for everyone to see.

Their lavish lifestyles are open for everyone to see. Nowhere is this more apparent than when hordes of private jets descend on luxurious destinations such as Davos,

Switzerland and Jackson Hole, Wyoming. Our
public servants, accompanied by their Wall
Street friends attend conferences to plot
their next moves to increase the power of the
cartel. All in the name of helping to create a
better economy for everyone. The results speak
for themselves. Attendees will spend more in a
few days than a family would pay to have a
wedding for a son or daughter. Is it any
wonder why our public servants fight so hard
to become part of this elite group?

This chapter is in no way intended to
imply all politicians and government employees
are involved in or agree with the cartel's
nefarious activities. I have to believe the
vast majority of government employees work
hard to do the right thing for the right
reason. Senators Paul and Warren are examples
of politicians fighting hard against the
cartel for the American public. Unfortunately,
the cartel holds the balance of power. In
fact, they are so large and powerful that I
needed to sub-title this chapter.

**How it Works**

In brief here is how it works. The Wall
Street banks, hedge funds and private equity
firms make enormous contributions to
politicians to the tune of billions of
dollars. Wall Street can also give high paying
jobs to ex-office holders and ex-employees of
governmental regulating agencies. On top of
that, the lucky few at the pinnacle of the
food chain can receive very generous speaking
fees to the tune of hundreds of thousands of
dollars per speech from Wall Street firms
after they leave government employment. One

has to include the Federal Reserve as a member in good standing of this cartel. No one really knows what the heck this organization truly is. Suffice it to say that they have thousands of employees with salaries totaling over a billion dollars and exert enormous influence over our citizens. These employees enjoy average salaries of over $70,000 per year, greatly exceeding the average salaries of the citizens they "serve".

So what does the Wall Street gang receive for their money? Enormous wealth and freedom from prosecution for criminal acts to start with. I don't have to go into a lot of detail on the income inequality in this country driven by the cartel. You see it and you feel it. A recent study showed that the wealthiest 62 people in the world had as much wealth as the poorest 3.6 billion people in the world. Read it again, it is not a typo. In case you think it doesn't matter, consider the following. Income inequality is the currently the worst it has been since the late 1920's which marked the start of the Great Depression. Kind of depressing isn't it! The Wall Street gang reels in huge amounts of booty as a result of our government's role in their activities. And you very, very rarely see one of them spend a day in jail as a result of their countless activities that break laws. Unbelievably a recent Attorney General of the United States as much as said that they are simply too big to prosecute for crimes.

### A Huge Scheme - The Housing Bubble

The Housing Bubble created by the cartel

is a perfect illustration. The cartel fueled a huge boom in housing during the last decade. Incalculable amounts of money were made by the Wall Street gang. The politicians were happy because jobs were being created and they were getting reelected. People were happy as their homes went up in value. They were encouraged to borrow freely against their homes from the banks and spend, spend, spend. They created "liar loans" and "NINJA"(no income no job no assets) loans. All the while our regulators turned a blind eye to newspaper headlines describing the situation. Fortunes were made and laws were broken. It was all a charade, organized by the cartel, that came crashing down on the heads of the American public. You know what happened next, millions of people lost their homes, bankers were thrown in jail, politicians were thrown out of office and regulators were fired. Err not exactly. Yes, millions of Americans did have their homes foreclosed and suffered greatly. The rest of the story worked out quite differently.

Wall Street executives continued to enjoy generous salaries and bonuses while their employees were being laid off left and right. Professional politicians continued to get reelected, after all who could have seen the bust coming. Regulators continued to receive their generous salaries at the expense of the very citizens that suffered from the bust. Ex-politicians and ex-regulators continued to get their cushy jobs and lavish speaking fees from Wall Street. The next member of the Wall Street gang that goes to jail for their part in illegal activities related to the housing scheme will be the first I have heard of. Similarly, the next regulator that gets fired for their actions or lack of action will also be the first I've heard of.

### The Wall Street Poster Child

For some reason the investment firm of Goldman Sachs seems to have become the poster child of the intertwined relationship between Wall Street and Washington. Here is just a tiny sample of some of the relationships:

- Goldman paid a current presidential candidate $675,000 for just 3 speeches,

- A current presidential candidate's wife is on leave from employment at Goldman,

-Several former Goldman chairmen have served as Treasury Secretary of the United States,

-Goldman has employed a multitude of former Securities and Exchange Commission public servants (the SEC is the "watchdog" of the securities industry),

-Former Goldman executives directed the efforts of the $700 billion Wall Street bailout,

-Goldman employees reputedly contributed more money to electing Obama than any other company,

-Goldman has dozens of ex-governmental employees on staff working as lobbyists,

-Former Federal Reserve officials have been employed or received speaking fees from

Goldman,

This list is just the tip of the iceberg but you get the idea. And Goldman is far from alone among Wall Street firms. The fox is guarding the Treasury hen-house. I can't emphasize enough how small a sample this list is. Just these few examples should be enough to cause anyone to wonder what the heck is going on here. Not to say Goldman is any better or worse that dozens of other firms but they may be the most visible. I can't judge the motives of the tens of thousands of people involved in these relationships over the years. I'm sure many positive things have resulted from the cross pollination of Washington and Wall Street.

## Crime and Punishment

What happens if the intertwined relationships are not so positive? The punishment for the gang members for their nefarious actions are merely fines. Hardly a person loses a job. The fines levied on the Wall Street gang have added up to over $40 billion dollars. The aforementioned Goldman Sacks has recently, reputedly, to have agreed to a $5 billion fine for their part in the housing bubble mortgage fraud scheme. Ok, so the bad guys got punished. Not so fast. First of all, the fines were paid primarily by their companies. Secondly, the profits they hauled in from their activities usually exceeded the fines. If fact billions in fines continue to be levied on the gang for various new and different nefarious activities since the housing bubble scheme. Once again they break the law and get fined for an amount less then they raked in. I think that fact that fines for new activities continue to happen tells us that they make a net profit on the activities after paying the fine.

Try stealing from a convenience store and see if you are simply asked to pay a fine in an amount less than what you stole instead of spending time in jail. What would stop someone from stealing more everyday if they only had to pay a fine for a lessor amount. Nice work if you can get it. That is how the game is played. That is the result of a completely corrupt government participating within a corrupt cartel. Now if you really want to get angry, consider that these fines are tax deductible. That's right, the fines are reduced by savings in taxes paid. As a bonus the professional politicians also get to claim they are doing their job by collecting these fines.

**The Federal Reserve**

The Federal Reserve's role in ongoing cartel activities is a bit harder to understand. Yes, they get their jobs and speaking fees from the investment gangs. They may turn a blind eye to nefarious activities. But the damage they do is systematic. The Federal Reserve is supposed to help keep inflation under control and help to create jobs - the "dual mandate". To give you an idea of how good a job they doing with inflation consider the following. If someone had one U.S. dollar at the inception of the Federal Reserve, it could now buy something worth one penny in today's economy. In other words, inflation has eaten away 99% of your buying power. Not so good. Bad news for you but good news for the cartel. It would take too long to explain why but I think the fact that Wall Street firms are raking in record profits is proof enough.

Want more proof? How about the fact that savers and the elderly are being punished by being paid virtually nothing in interest on their life's savings while the gang prospers? The Federal Reserve is pushing savers into risky Wall Street schemes that inevitably collapse and leave them holding the bag. If the gang just needs to park some of the loot from savers' zero interest bank and money market deposits, the Fed will gladly pay the gang interest on your money. There is even talk of "negative interest rates" where you will have to pay the banks for the privilege of them hanging onto your money. Just doesn't smell right does it?

The recent oil boom engineered by the cartel is a current example. Oil prices have been driven to record high prices, made possible by the availability of free money. Huge amounts of savers money are then pushed into the hands of the cartel for risky energy investment schemes. Then the price of oil collapses causing huge losses to the unwary investors. They have also been hard at work on an automobile bubble. Drive sales of autos to record numbers by the availability of easy, cheap loans. Expand the terms of the loans to 8 years making payments lower. Finance the auto, the sales taxes and fees, generous trade in allowances plus a cash bonus for buying the car. The end result is a consumer driving out the door with a 5 to 8-year loan in an amount 20%-40% more than what they could sell the car for. Just like the housing bubble the financial companies make a fortune and the consumers will be crying in their Toyota in a few years. Rinse and repeat. Who knows what will be next.

We haven't even discussed derivatives. Derivatives is a fancy word for made up financial assets of almost unlimited varieties like swaps, forwards, options and so on. The nominal amount of derivatives could exceed some quadrillion dollars. A quadrillion is 1,000 trillion. No one knows how much for certain since it is a complex, and for the most part unregulated market. This has only been made possible by Central Banks around the world creating the liquidity conditions that enable unlimited derivatives to be created. A well-known billionaire investor has likened them to a time bomb and weapons of mass destruction. While a former Federal Reserve Chairman has stated that the derivatives market has become so large because it provides economic value to their users. The users in this case would be the cartel. If this baby blows up it is game over. It won't matter who you vote for. Trump has said that he would demand to know just what the Federal Reserve is up to.

### The Great Job Killing Machine

The cartel has become a great job killing machine. Regulations driven by special interests of all flavors are strangling economic enterprise in this country. The regulations make it difficult for businesses to create or keep jobs in this country. The regulations have helped to drive growth to a standstill in this country, with growth being picked up by less regulated countries like China. The regulatory war on Americans has driven up the cost of everything made in America that we consume or use. Meanwhile wages are decreasing as businesses can no longer compete if they have to pay a living wage to American workers.

In light of decreasing or declining domestic growth the cartel has adjusted. The cartel needs higher stock and investment prices to thrive. The Federal Reserve plays a critical role in this scheme. The centerpiece of the solution is to print tons of money and price it at zero. The Federal Reserve has done just that. The gang members and corporations can borrow money at virtually zero interest rates. By the way, that means you receive a zero interest return on your savings. This free money is the gas that powers the scheme. Sadly, this gas was previously used in measured amounts to drive job creation.

Jobs as a percentage of the population are declining. They can make up any statistics they want such as the very manipulated unemployment rate. That doesn't change the fact that fewer working age Americans are working full-time than at any time in decades. And many of those who want to work are only able to get part-time jobs. A mass of regulations has helped to fuel part-time employment. The mother of which is Obamacare. Whatever else Obamacare has accomplished, it has thrown many people into part-time employment. It is simply too much cheaper for corporations under Obamacare to employ part-time workers.

Using only stock prices as an example, I will roughly outline how the free money scheme works to kill jobs. Even as the free money fuel has recently driven stock prices to record highs it applies to other types of investments as well. Wall Street packages "free" money in the form of debt that corporations issue. Much of this debt issued by corporations is called "covenant lite", meaning the borrowing conditions are less strict thereby reducing the chances that it can be paid back. This covenant lite debt sets the stage for yet another bailout by the public. The money received from the debt is then used to buy back the corporation's own stock. The amount of stock outstanding is reduced therefore the price of the stock goes up. Additionally, regulators allow companies to deceive the public about how much money they actually earn. Companies are freely allowed to tout to investors their "adjusted earnings". Adjusted earnings are shorthand for excluding many costs of doing business. Therefore, earnings look higher than they actually are from a historical perspective. Once again stock prices go up without the need for growth or jobs.

Companies are also shifting jobs to other countries to take advantage of lower labor costs. Labor costs are lower in other countries for many reasons. People will work for less because their cost of living is less. A significant and direct reason relates to the regulations that are killing jobs in this country. In many countries companies can employ people without regard to workers' health care, safety of their working environment and their age and hours worked per day. Also, companies don't need to worry about the environmental impact of their factories. The list of regulations they escape is as endless as the millions of pages of regulations in this country. Companies earn more profits and stock prices go up by shifting jobs elsewhere. The ugly truth is that the regulations we care so deeply about can be avoided by moving American jobs to other countries.

The latest innovation out of Wall Street is an activity called "Inversions". Many countries have lower income tax rates than we do. Many American companies are now shifting their legal headquarters to other countries. They do this by buying or merging with the foreign company. They then move numbers of corporate employees to the foreign country. This inversion results in the company paying less in taxes. Earnings go up and likewise stock prices go up. Jobs in America go down along with our tax receipts from corporations. Trump has said he will stop inversions in two seconds.

## Politicians Have Their Back.

The damage done to our financial system by the cartel is enormous. By creating yet another stock market bubble we are setting the stage for another bailout. Our professional politicians regularly bail out the banks and corporations like General Motors after every scheme blows up. These bailouts amount to hundreds of billions of dollars. There is no incentive for the gang to change if there are no consequences for failure. Our politicians are the enablers of these schemes. The professional politicians refuse to reel in the activities of the secretive Federal Reserve. They allow the Federal Reserve to manipulate interest rates and create enormous amounts of money for two primary reasons. First, it allows the Wall Street gang to create massive wealth for themselves. Secondly, it allows the government to borrow money cheaply.

The politicians can also spend more if it costs less in interest to borrow the money on the debt they ring up. If we paid just 1% more on our $19 trillion in debt that would be $190 billion more of interest we would pay. And that additional interest would get added to new debt every year. If we paid 2% more, that would amount to $380 billion every year. Now you get the idea why the professional politicians want us to earn nothing on our savings.

### Everybody's Talking About the Good Old Days

It didn't always used to be this way. Banks have been an integral contributor to our economic strength. They made sound loans that helped borrowers prosper and create jobs. I think it is fair to say that we wouldn't be an economic powerhouse without them. This was accomplished with primarily local and regional banks. They were smaller, close to the people and did not exert control over federal government officials. They expected to be repaid for the loans they made. The old style local and regional banks are now in the process of being driven out of business as a result of the burdens of the back breaking government regulations imposed upon them. Their activities are being consolidated in the hands of the Wall Street gang that can afford to pay for the costs of regulations. As smaller banks disappear the circle of corruption is being expanded.

## Can and Will Even The Donald Change it

The simple answer is that he alone cannot disarm the cartel of mass destruction if he is elected president. He can begin to sanitize it. But he and he alone among active candidates has unique attributes that would allow him to make a difference. Once again he is self-funding. He has also dealt with the stifling governmental regulations firsthand as a large business owner. He knows the dangers to our way of life from over-regulation. He knows the cartel game inside and out. He has bought influence from politicians of all flavors. Nothing quite sums it up as his answer as to why Mrs. Clinton was at his wedding. "She really had no choice because I gave to a foundation." Trump has operated within the highest levels of the elites. He can speak their language.

The fact that he will owe no one favors for donations and that he is so accomplished and experienced in the ways of big money give him an edge. He does not need lucrative speaking fees or donations to a family foundation. He is already rich. He does not need to resist the temptations of the cartel; he is not even tempted to begin with. Of all

the candidates he is the only one that has
created a very large, successful job-creating
international enterprise. Trump could not have
accomplished what he has without spending
wisely unlike our professional politicians
that have rung up $19 trillion in debt.

If you don't think a rich Republican
would really look out for the average guy,
consider Republican President Teddy Roosevelt.
He was born into a wealthy family but went on
to become the original progressive President.
He championed a "Square Deal" policy for the
average American. After failing to win the
reelection primary he even formed his own
progressive party. It can be done and it has
been done.

Wall Street, our government employees and
our corporate leaders stand ready to build a
job creating machine if only our system would
encourage them. Trump would unleash our best
and brightest to do just that.

# Not Skating on By

"Life's most persistent and urgent
question is,
'What are you doing for others?'"

Martin Luther King, Jr.


Sometimes a person does something that simply deserves a separate chapter. Where a person made a decision to do something just because it was the right thing to do. Where a person didn't just carry on with their life and ignore an opportunity to help others. Didn't just keep skating on by. The summer of 1986 was just such a time. The Wollman Memorial Skating Rink renovation was just such an opportunity. Donald Trump didn't just keep skating.

The Wollman Ice-Rink in Central Park, New York City, had been mired in a failed government-led renovation for the past six years. They had spent over $13 million dollars during the six years and still had not been able to renovate an ice-skating rink! The project had originally been estimated to cost $9 million dollars and take two years to complete. New estimates to complete the renovations were at a cost of $2.5-$3 million dollars and were again estimated to take two years. The rink was a treasured part of Central Park. It had been utilized as a place ordinary people could go to have fun and relax. An oasis in the midst of the concrete jungle of the big city. A place were families could shrug off the stresses of everyday life. All at an affordable price. But alas, it laid unused.

It was then that Trump stopped skating and wrote a letter to the Mayor of New York City, Mr. Koch. In the letter Trump offered to finish the rink by the end of the year. In the letter he stated that he had built Trump Tower in 26 months and that he saw no reason the rink couldn't be completed in four months. He also offered to operate the rink and turn over any profits to charities. The City had expected the rink to generate losses as opposed to profits. Trump disagreed. After intense negotiations between Trump and the Mayor, an agreement was reached where Trump would complete the project and manage the rink.

In November of 1986 the beautifully renovated Wollman Memorial Rink reopened! It was completed at a cost that was $750,000 under budget and ahead of schedule. In April of 1987 it was reported that the rink netted a profit of $400,000-$500,000. The City had expected significant losses to be incurred operating the Rink. A record number of 225,000 people were able to enjoy the rink at an affordable cost of $4.50 during its first season. And it was beautiful!

As of April, 1987 money from the profits of that first season had been allocated as follows:

$25,000 for the Partnership for the

Homeless

$25,000 for United Cerebral Palsy

$25,000 for the Gay Men's Health Crisis

$75,000 to renovate a playground in each of the 5 boroughs of the city

More donations to various charities were to follow.

All of this because one man wanted people to have a skating rink.

# Building a Wall with Legos

"It is not in the stars to hold our
destiny but in ourselves"

William Shakespeare


Let's just get the physical construction
of the wall question out of the way. Trump
building a wall on a mostly wasteland southern
boarder would be like your child playing with
Legos. Anyone who would have you believe that
it is impossible or impractical to build a
wall is simply not telling the truth or is
naively unaware of great American
accomplishments. Until a wall is built we will
not control the destiny of our country. If you
need proof, you simply need to examine wall-
less Europe becoming overwhelmed by crime and
terror for masses of "refugees".

The following are words spoken by
President Franklin D. Roosevelt 80 years ago
at the Dedication of the Boulder (later the
Hoover) dam.

"We are here to celebrate the completion
of the greatest dam in the world, rising 726
feet above the bedrock of the river and
altering the geography of a whole region: we
are here to see the creation of the largest

artificial lake in the world-115 miles long, holding enough water, for example, to cover the whole State of Connecticut to a depth of ten feet; and we are here to see nearing completion a power house which will contain the largest generators and turbines yet installed in this country, machinery that can continuously supply nearly two million horsepower of electric energy."

President Franklin D. Roosevelt continued, "This morning I came, I saw, and I was conquered, as everyone would be who sees for the first time this great feat of mankind. . .. Ten years ago the place where we gathered was an unpeopled, forbidding desert. In the bottom of the gloomy canyon whose precipitous walls rose to heights of more than a thousand feet, flowed a turbulent, dangerous river. . . . The site of Boulder City was a cactus-covered waste. And the transformation wrought here in these years is a twentieth century marvel." Speech by Roosevelt at the Dedication of Boulder Dam, September 30, 1935.

I have stood on the top of this dam and it is stunning. Words alone cannot explain the absolute scope and scale of this American accomplishment. A feeling of awe overtook me as I stood on top of 3,250,000 cubic yards of concrete almost 100 stories high above the largest water reservoir in the country. This dam was constructed in just 5 years. Keep in mind that this was during the 1930s. We had no computers and none of our modern mammoth construction equipment. By the way it only cost $49 million to complete.

I have also stood at the top of the

Empire State Building. It also offers a breath-taking view. This building was completed 85 years ago in 1931. It took less than two years to build at a cost of $41,000,000. It stands 102 stories, has 73 elevators and at the time was the tallest building in the world. Once again there were no computers to aid in the design, planning and construction of this magnificent building. There were not the modern cranes and other equipment to use during the construction. Amazing.

On September 12, 1962, President John F. Kennedy famously said during a speech "We choose to go to the moon". Seven years later on July 20, 1969 Apollo 11 became the first manned mission to land on the moon. How's that for American "can do" attitude in action.

All three of these great American accomplishments created tens of thousands of American jobs. They were examples of our "can do" attitude, imagination and innovation. They were completed many years ago without the technological advantages we currently enjoy. Please don't feel people are so stupid as to believe we can't build a wall. If we choose not to build a wall on our southern border it is quite simply because we don't want to do it.

# He has no Experience, OH NO!

"First they ignore you, then they laugh at you, then they fight you, then you win"

Mahatma Gandhi

Yippee! That is a one-word answer to those who knock Trump for not having experience as a professional politician. We have elected to the presidency one professional politician after another. Do you feel better off because of it? Trump would tell you that professional politicians are a big reason we are in the mess we are in. We've elected professional politicians for decades, how's that working out for you? One definition of "insanity" is continuing to do the same thing over and over but expecting a different result. Isn't that what we have been doing? Trump is shouting - stop the madness! And people are listening. Americans may be crazy but most of us aren't insane. So yes, when people scream that Trump has no experience as a professional politician a lot of people are shouting - Yippee!

The following reflects what I believe to be a simple example of the difference between a professional politician and a person who desires to serve our country. When the Power-Ball lottery recently reached the fantastic sum of $1.5 billion dollars it garnered enormous attention. Trump was asked what he would do with the money if he won. He immediately replied that he would give it to our veterans. Hillary Clinton was asked the same question. It took her a while to come up with a worthwhile cause but ultimately she said that she would fund her campaign. One person is a professional politician, one is not. I'm not sure what else to say about that. Some people are generous with your money and others are generous with theirs. "For where your treasure is, there your heart will be also", Luke 12:34.

So what is Trump if he is not an "experienced" politician? He is a person who took what he had and turned it into a wildly successful multi-billion-dollar international enterprise. Critics will say that Trump had an advantage because his family had money therefore he had a great education and the other perks of being born into a wealthy family. Hard to argue with that. There is a baseball saying for people who had such an advantage and rest on their laurels - he was born on third base and thought he hit a triple. Trump may have been born on third base but he didn't just stand on third base and rest on his laurels. He kept coming back to the plate and hit home-run after home-run. That is taking your God given talents and making the most of them. By his own calculations he is worth billions of dollars.

Trump is the Chief Executive Officer(CEO) of a vast array of successful enterprises.

That means he is the person vested with the ultimate responsibility for the success or failure of the organization. That is just about as close as you can get to the definition of the President of the United States. When we elect a President, we in effect hire a President. In the non-governmental world people aren't hired for positions because they really, really want to be. They are hired primarily because of their ability to do the job. Americans have gotten into the habit of hiring(electing) people based on how bad they want it and their ability to raise money and make good speeches. As an example, no large non-governmental enterprise in the world would hire a person whose main accomplish was "community organizing" to be their CEO. We just did that, twice, to run our country! Now, as Trump would say, we have a mess.

Our government is the vastest man-made organization on the planet earth. We need someone who can process the enormous complexities of our government. We need someone who can juggle activities related to our military, congress, the media, foreign leaders, the needs of our citizens and much more. That person should also be able to make agreements requiring compromises with various parties that may not see eye to eye with each other. We need a person that can hire competent employees, inspire them and lead them to success. We need a person who can communicate effectively with us and people around the world. Many of us want a President that will build on what we have and make America greater that what it already is. Our president should have strong Judeo-Christian values, even if they are not a Christian, unless we chose to scrap all that has made us great and start over. Although this is a partial list you get the idea.

There are also important character qualifications in being a president. On top of the list are trustworthiness and honesty. A CEO/President's actions filter throughout an entire organization. If they are dishonest or not trustworthy then everyone in the organization will feel free to follow their example. We have historically been a transparent nation of laws and open government. The president has the responsibility for the enforcement of our laws. This is not to be confused with making our laws. That is clearly the responsibility of congress. Consider if we elected a president that was not honest or trustworthy. The president and his employees would feel free to lie to us and cover-up their activities. They would also feel free to ignore the enforcement of laws they didn't agree with. They would also feel free to apply their own interpretation to laws and punitively enforce them against people they didn't like. They could lie to congress about their actions. Kind of scary huh?

Let's take a hypothetical example that I'm sure everyone can relate to, the IRS. Say for example we had an administration that played by their own rules. Say they didn't like one particular group of citizens that were political rivals and the IRS employees felt empowered to treat that group unfairly. Well, no problem, you would say. We would simply have the appropriate regulators investigate these unfair practices and then discipline any employees who had applied the laws unjustly. Ah, but what if we had a president that agreed with these unlawful actions. What if the employees destroyed evidence of wrongdoing such as computer storage devices? What if the offending employees were not disciplined? What if the employees lied to regulators and congress about their actions? Imagine if you took this hypothetical example and multiplied it by a million actions by our government employees. Even imagine if we had partisan Cabinet Members who decided they could hide or destroy their correspondence or emails to keep their activities hidden. Kind of chilling isn't it?

If our standard for president was perfection, there wouldn't be any viable candidates. How does Trump stack up on honesty and trustworthiness? I have never met the man therefore I can only go by what his actions have displayed. Vetted is a popular word in "media-speak". Vetting is the process of performing a background check on someone before offering them employment. How well has Trump been vetted? As outlined below, Trump has had very significant business activities throughout the world.

In order to accomplish his business objectives, he would have had to be in compliance with hundreds of thousands, if not millions, of laws and regulations. He would have had to work with thousands and thousands of regulating agencies throughout the world regarding building codes, environmental, safety, financial stability and a myriad of such issues. He would have had to file

millions of pages of documents to various
agencies. It gives me a headache just thinking
about it! He would have had untold numbers of
loan agreements and disclosures to banks
throughout the world. Banks may be the most
highly regulated corporate entities in the
world. In essence, if he is dealing with them
he is also subject to be being reviewed by the
banks' regulators. His activities would be
scrutinized by other parties he would deal
with. A partial list would include unions,
utilities and civil rights groups. I doubt
there could be a more stringent vetting
process than he has experienced in his
business activities. He has done all of this
successfully. If he were a crook or a liar he
surely would have been outed as such,
particularly given his high profile in the
media. Well, he is still standing!

There is the issue of several
bankruptcies involving a casino bearing his
name. This was not a personal bankruptcy.
Trump did not ever file for personal
bankruptcy as some of his detractors would
have you believe. It is beyond the scope of
this book to get into all the details. That
would require an entire book to describe.
Bankruptcy is part of the legal structure in
our country. If done in the proper manner it
is a legal personal and business activity.
Bankruptcy in our country has been viewed as a
necessary part of our legal system. Centuries
ago in England people who could not pay their
debts were thrown into "debtors prisons" until
they could pay. As you can imagine, not many
debtors paid their debts from prison.

We as a country have decided that is

appropriate to have an option for people and corporations to file bankruptcy. Imagine if you could, if the millions of people in this country who have filed for bankruptcy were rotting away in prisons until they could repay their debts. Doesn't sound like a very workable system. To be clear many innocent people are harmed by a bankruptcy. But that doesn't make people who file for bankruptcy immoral or criminals. It is neither rare nor unusual for people or corporations to file for bankruptcy. Trump has had a handful of his organizations file for bankruptcy out of probably thousands he has controlled. What would you expect him to do, voluntarily show up at the door of a prison? He has endured times where he has struggled financially but has bounced back stronger than ever. Isn't that what our country needs right now?

So, is Trump qualified to be president? What has he actually done to demonstrate that he is capable of being the most important CEO in the world? Trump has built or controlled skyscrapers all over the world including New York City, Chicago, Vancouver, Florida, Istanbul, Dubai, Brazil, Uruguay, and the Philippines to name some. He controls a portfolio of golf courses in the U.S., the U.K. and Dubai. He has built a media empire that includes TV shows such as The Apprentice and beauty pageants. He manages an ice skating rink in Central Park, NYC. He has written over a dozen successful books. He has a merchandise portfolio that includes clothing among other items. I am sure I have missed some of his accomplishments but you get the idea. His list of business accomplishments rivals anything I have ever seen considering its size, diversity of activities and geographical reach. It is also important to recognize he has done this profitably. What does this say about Trump's ability to manage a complex organization such as the U.S. Government? His accomplishments clearly indicate he is qualified beyond a reasonable doubt.

Anyone who thinks government can do most things better than private enterprises just isn't paying attention. In 2011 a popular baseball film, MONEYBALL, was released. It documented the efforts of the Oakland A's small-market baseball team general manager, played by Brad Pitt, to rebuild his team quickly and on a limited budget. The baseball "experts" ridiculed his efforts. In the end he was wildly successful. He used his limited dollars to sign the best baseball players he could afford based on their performance. He didn't follow the old rules that paid enormous amounts of money to experienced players based on their reputation. He won the same number of games as the New York Yankees at a cost of $264,000 per player versus the Yankee's cost of $1,400,000 per player. The government reminds me of the baseball's New York Yankees. Private enterprise reminds me of a small city baseball team. Following this example, Trump would represent the general manager of the Oakland A's and experienced governmental officials would represent the Yankees. (Please don't confuse me with Ted Cruz, this analogy is not meant to insult the people of New York or the Yankees.) It is simply to provide a relate-able analogy. Like the Oakland A's, Trump would hire the best people to do the job we need done at the lowest cost possible.

# Yea he Changed his Mind, Haven't you?

"There are two kinds of fools: Those who can't change their opinions and those who won't."

Josh Billings

One of the criticisms leveled at Trump is the fact that he has changed his mind on some issues over the years. He has also changed his political party. I can't believe one single American has never changed their opinion on many things over their lifetime. In fact, we are known as an adaptable culture. That trait is one of the attributes that has made our country great.

I started life as a Democrat, then I was a Republican and now I am neither. I don't feel the need to apologize. I was a Democrat at 18 for practical reasons. The city I lived in was controlled by the Democrats. When my older brother registered as a Republican our property taxes promptly went up. From then on we were all Democrats and our taxes went back down. I became a Republican because they were fiscally conservative. When they stopped being fiscally conservative I dumped them also. Real life choices made by one person. Doesn't any candidate face the same choices?

Changing your beliefs is not the same as changing what you say. It is not the same as "I was for it before I was against it" as in the case of the Iraq war. If you are now against war and that is why you changed your mind, fine. If you still believe in interventionist wars and nation building, then that is different. You have simply realized that in the case of that particular war it didn't work out so it was a mistake. You are simply admitting you made a mistake in that particular case. Trump was originally against that war because he didn't believe it was the right thing to do. He still feels that way.

People change their minds for all kinds of reasons. The advancement of science, personal experiences, growing older and dramatic life events are a few of the reasons. Some people say early in life that they don't want to have children. Yet as they age they change their minds. Someone might have wanted a bigger, more expensive house. Yet after the housing bubble they may never want it. A person may have believed in an aggressive foreign policy. Maybe they lose a loved one in a war and change their mind. Someone may have believed that a certain disease could spread by touch. But then after medical science evolved they knew it was not true.

Trump has been criticized for changing his views on abortion. He has said his change of opinion was due to a personal experience. Who can judge what is in a person's heart? Only their speech and actions provide but an imperfect window. Consistency from the moment of change is a "tell" as they say in poker.

Professional politicians have become adept at playing to the crowd. They say one thing to a crowd in one state and a different thing to a crowd in another state. That is not a change in opinion, it is deception. They may change their stated beliefs based on opinion polls, not on what they believe. That is not a personal opinion change. That is an expedient action in an effort to get votes. Pundits call it flip-flopping. Once again, who can say which is which? Trump has appeared to me as a normal person who has changed some of his opinions over time.

# Freely Trading Away Your Jobs

"The world's a mean place, It's unfair, then it's fair. It's hateful, then it's loving. It's a very peculiar place on philosophical and metaphysical and religious levels."
Tim Allen

Trump has spoken quite a bit about China so I will focus on this particular country. How are we doing in our trade with China? China sells over $300-500 billion dollars more of products to us every year than we sell to them. Not so good. It has been estimated we have lost 3,000,000-5,000,000 jobs as a result of trading with China alone. And this number would probably vastly understate the jobs we lost. As a result of our trade with China we now owe them over $1.2 trillion dollars! We trade our future for their cheap labor. Sounds fair to me. Make no mistake, the special interests have created this imbalance. Large U.S. companies love the cheap labor. Banks make fortunes off the loans to finance this trade. Our business leaders would love to make the products and create jobs here but they can't afford to under our corrupt system.

Our trade agreements are negotiated in the private, expensive meetings and dinners attended by our professional politicians. Not to worry, of courses the politicians consult with their large donors to make sure we get a fair deal. The professional politicians are hard at work on their latest sell out of American workers. It's called the Trans-Pacific Partnership(TTP). It is being negotiated in secret, not unlike Obamacare, and we know how that worked out. Our prior Secretary of State, Mrs. Clinton, even made the TTP deal a high priority, although that may have changed now with votes on the line. That is how it works, I love it for the contributions but no wait, I'm not so sure about it with workers votes on the line. Never mind, just elect me and I'll work it out in private.

Meanwhile, China blocks U.S. companies at every turn from selling our products into their country. Ask anyone who tries to sell products into China. Our government will tell you, sure but, we sell billions worth of products to China. This is true but much of what we sell to China is repackaged and sold right back to us. China pirates our technology and hacks our computers. There have even been stores in China that look exactly like Apple stores but are entirely counterfeit right down to the Logos. Our government response is similar to a pet dog that rolls over on its back expecting to be scratched. That a boy.

So why is it cheaper to make products in China? Let's start with the workers. They are barely paid subsistence wages. They are packed in living quarters like rats. They include young children. They have working conditions reminiscent of the brutal conditions in a Victorian era Dickens novel. If they complain they can be replaced in a heartbeat by any of millions of others waiting to get a job. Although this is not true of all Chinese manufacturers it is true enough for too many to ignore.

I have belonged to six unions in my life. Why any union worker, not employed by the government, would vote for anyone but Trump is beyond me. Politicians of both parties have been killing jobs in this country for decades in the name of free trade. And the jobs we have lost have been replaced by workers in other countries under working conditions contrary to everything unions represent. In addition, wages for union and non-union workers in America have been driven down in a quest to compete with cheap foreign labor. American workers can barely eke out a living.

How about the environment that we care so deeply about? What is this "free trade" doing to the environment of the world? The air in the capital city of China, Beijing, is so polluted you practically need to wear night vision glasses in the middle of the day just to see. But have no fear. Obama negotiated a global warming deal with China to solve this problem. Interestingly, on the very day Chinese officials were bragging about meeting Obama's goals they had to shut down activity in Beijing because the air pollution was so high. Meanwhile back at home, jobs are being lost to hold up our part of the deal. Their water is unsafe to drink in many areas of the country. It has been estimated that over 70% of rivers and lakes in China are polluted by industrial activities. But you get the idea. Our jobs are being sent to other countries that don't have to follow our environmental laws. Our environmental laws add a significant cost to business activity in this country. We have decided that regulations are important, but only in this country.

We have extensive product safety laws in this country. These range from food ingredients to physical products such as baby strollers. It is cheaper to make virtually everything we consume or utilize in our daily lives if safety is not a concern. It can be cheaper if ingredients or materials used are unsafe or substandard. It is cheaper if products are cheaply designed. As high as 50% of the products recalled in America were imported from China. These range from toothpaste to lead covered toys to dog food. The dog food issue is particularly troubling. How are dogs expected to protect themselves? I have been forced to carefully scrutinize dog food to make sure that they are not made in China using dangerous chemicals. And it is not easy to determine where a product is really made. You have to carefully search the fine print on the labels. Even so, country of origin can be cleverly disguised.

In the case of food and product safety our government does try to monitor imports for violations of our safety laws. Unfortunately, it is a daunting task to completely protect us against producers that intentionally subvert our laws. In this country executives that intentionally subverted our safety laws would go to jail. In China they would buy another Porsche.

Chinese companies are showered with

government loans. Many of these loans would never be made if they were expected to be paid back. But the goal of government loans in China appears to be the creation of jobs rather than the return of the money loaned. In essence, these loans represent free money used to produce products for export thereby creating Chinese jobs. They have also kept their currency below it's true value. These policies put products manufactured in the U.S. at a competitive cost disadvantage. Goodbye jobs. Of course our companies get some financing assistance from our government as well but this assistance pales in comparison to Chinese financing subsidies. China has created a debt bubble that will make our housing bubble look like a picnic in the park when it explodes. And our Federal Reserve has enabled this situation with their free money policies. Trump has often spoken out against China's unfair practices.

I agree with Trump that the Chinese are good people. They are simply doing what they allowed to do by their government, and ours, to make a living. In fact, more millionaires are being created in China than anywhere else in the world. They are obviously very talented. There have been many positive results from our trade with China but they have come at a cost. They have systematically accumulated billions of wealth every year at our expense. International trade is a very important part of our daily lives. But as Trump has said, it needs to be fair. Currently "free trade" is nothing but a sell-out of American citizens.

Trump is not an isolationist. He has

built many projects in countries all over the world. He obviously appreciates international trade and feels comfortable dealing with foreign citizens and countries. I have no doubt Trump would work hard to even the playing field for American workers while providing opportunities for foreign interests. If elected using no special interest money, he would owe nothing to anyone but the American people. He is a master negotiator and even wrote a bestselling book - The Art of The Deal. In the book he talks about a key part of fair agreements being the courage to walk away from a bad deal. As president I have no doubt he would walk away from any deal that was bad for the American public. That is how he has operated his entire successful career. In any case it is hard to imagine he could do worse than what we have now.

# Trump's Finger on the Button

"Those who do not remember the past are condemned to repeat it."

George Santayana


You may have heard pundits asking - do we really want Trump's finger on the nuclear button? They kind of wink and chuckle as if to say - you all know we really need an experienced professional in charge. The following are some of the major foreign policy challenges managed by our experienced professionals over the last 16 years.

History will show that we have made two critical foreign policy blunders of historic proportions during the last 16 years. That is two full terms by two politician presidents. These presidents were different in many ways but similar in the most fateful ways. Neither understood history, or the costs and consequences of their actions. The first blunder, committed by President Bush, was attacking Iraq. The second blunder, committed by President Obama, was rushing out of Iraq and leaving a murderous Iranian puppet in charge. Both these decisions were made by experienced politicians and their advisers. Donald Trump spoke out against both actions.

The Middle East has been a powder-keg for centuries. During the entire period of recorded history, the Middle East has been mired in regional wars. Iran and Iraq lost millions of solders fighting each other just a few decades ago. The glue that held the keg together were strong regional leaders who counter-balanced each other while controlling their restless and impoverished citizens. They became "made-up" Nations to begin with. People with different cultures, languages, religions, and allegiances thrown together by western bureaucrats playing with maps after wars that they had won. Neither president seemed to understand this basic history. Their decisions were a breathtaking display of naivety.

The decision to invade Iraq was made during a time when we had suffered a horrendous terrorist attack by radical Muslims. Undoubtedly, emotions played some part in that decision. That is understandable. According to the official reason out of Washington, we went into Iraq because they had weapons of mass destruction(WMDs). This turned out to be faulty, we found no WMDs. Once again these decisions were based on the opinions of "experts". I think we all realize the pain, suffering and loss of life that has occurred as a result. The estimated cost will probably exceed $2 trillion by the time all the costs are incurred.

The decision to pack up and high-tail it out of Iraq must have been a purely political decision. I refuse to believe we could have elected a president who would be so naive as to believe things would work out if we left a vast oil rich territory, inhabited by armed gangs, with no one in real control. Obama promised to pull out of Iraq and he did. He left the keys with a puppet dictator who was handpicked by the rulers of Iran. A fateful mistake was made to keep an election promise that was made years prior. The result is a brutal Iraqi government that is supported by tens of billions of our dollars. They are committing thousands of atrocious crimes and murders against their own people. In fact, the people of Iraq voted to democratically change this government and the Obama administration decided they liked the murderous Iranian puppet Maliki better, so we kept him in control. So much for supporting democracy.

Management 101 would teach anyone that when circumstances change, actions should change. Unfortunately, we had a community activist as president. The administration claimed Iraq did not want us there so we had no choice but to leave. At the same time, we send them tens of billions of dollars to use as they wish. It seems logical that had we told them - no U.S. airbase, no money - that we would have had an airbase. Had we had an airbase in Iraq, ISIS would have been wiped out in a New York minute as the Donald might say. Instead we have created an environment in which ISIS can thrive. But not to worry they are only a "J.V. team" according to our president.

Apparently we liked the results of our government overthrow in Iraq so much we decided to expand our efforts. Our administration encouraged the "Arab Spring". It should have been called the "Arab Hell". We encouraged the overthrow of leaders in countries such as Egypt and Libya to name just two. Terror now reigns in these countries. Almost uncountable numbers of their citizens are being tortured and murdered on a daily basis. People who wish harm to the rest of the world are growing more and more powerful every day. No small part of the blame rests with western powers intervention into a relativity stable Middle East, turning it into the wild, wild west. For our part, we have an administration filled with political operatives that see the world as they want to see it, rather than as it truly is. They ignore history and reality. They are like a bunch of children blissfully playing in a sand box full of fire ants. I haven't even mentioned Africa where Boko Haram extremists recently killed 86 people in Nigeria, including children burned to death. The 6-year Islamic uprising has killed over 20,000 people and left 2,500,000 people homeless in Nigeria alone.

It would be difficult to ignore the death of four Americans in Benghazi when thinking about who would make a good president. Four people, employed by the U.S. government, were brutally murdered on foreign soil at an American facility. They were stranded without support from the most powerful military in the world for hours upon hours. With deleted emails and evasive answers at investigative hearings we may never know why. One thing I am confident of is - if Donald Trump was president at the time, help would have arrived sooner than it did. The root cause of these deaths was the wildly celebrated Arab Spring. Libya fell into chaos and their stockpile of sophistical weapons fell into the hands of terrorists. We had people there trying to destroy those weapons before they could be used on us. We also had diplomats there pretending everything was peaches and crème. The politically correct thing to do I guess.

Probably the major foreign policy "achievement" of the Obama administration is the Iran deal. We agreed to give them $150 billion and end economic sanctions against them. They agreed to let us know if they keep working on nuclear bombs. They are using these funds to build bombs, support terrorism and buy airplanes from Europe. They continue to pledge the total destruction of Israel, fund terrorism around the world and destroy the American way of life. Only a miracle will prevent Iran from obtaining nuclear weapons under this agreement. Of course we don't know for sure because the American people don't know the details of the agreements. Only the people directly involved know their true motivations for agreeing to this deal. A nuclear Iran that is committed to the destruction of us and its neighbors will be the result of this deal. What exactly is our current administration committed to? Trump has made it clear that he is committed to our safety and I believe him. There is no need for a military button to be pushed if peaceful resolution is negotiated before it is too late.

It is not only our foreign policy actions that will have negative implications for our future. It is our inaction as well. As our administrations have slept, China is building air force bases on atolls in the oil-rich

South China Sea. They are claiming control over vast expanses of ocean used as the highways of ocean trade. They have ignored other countries' sovereign claims over these atolls. This has resulted in much friction among the countries involved. Once China completes its control over these vast areas of ocean it will be virtually impossible to peacefully reverse course. Not our business you might say. A student of history would say - not so fast. It was only 70 years ago we were attacked by Japan as part of their effort to conquer the entire western pacific. Japan's actions cost us dearly in American lives and treasure.

Trump has spoken out forcefully about China. He feels that we have let China dominate us in trade. He considers them smart and feels they aggressively take advantage of our "stupid" leaders. He is correct. They are doing what is good for them, not us. Who can blame them. Trump understands that China is primarily dependent on trade with America for its growing economy and thereby its domestic tranquility. We have allowed China to enjoy an "anything goes" relationship with us. They can dump their products on us while keeping their markets closed to our goods. They can pirate our brands and ignore our laws. They can build islands out of atolls in disputed territories for military bases. Trump fully understands that their economic dependence on us would allow peaceful negotiations regarding the South China Seas issue.

North Korea launched a long range missile around the time of the New Hampshire Republican debate. The candidates were asked if they would preemptively destroy North Korean missiles before they could carry out nuclear attacks. All the candidates, except Trump, talked at length about what military action we should or should not take. They stayed on point as if military action by us was the only solution. Trump's answer was the clearest indication I have seen that he understands the world better than any of them. That he thinks differently. He correctly stated that North Korea was basically controlled by the Chinese. He said that we should pressure China to put an end to the nuclear threat from the North Koreans.

Trump didn't need rooms full of policy wonks to explain to him the realities of the world we live in. North Korea is dependent on China for their very survival. China's economy is dependent on American trade. Demand that China solve the problem. Keep our finger away from the button! Clear, knowledgeable, realistic thinking on his part. As an aside, North Korea got to this point in developing nuclear weapons because of the Clinton administration. In a deal eerily similar to the Iran deal, we paid them not to develop nuclear weapons. Like with Iran, we were to trust them. One does not need to be a fortune teller to see where we will be with Iran in a few years.

Russia has become much more active in world affairs of late. They have a very weak economy therefore their impact on the world is not as great as it once was. Our relationship with them is still of great importance. They recently said our relationship with them has regressed back to the 1962 level of animosity.

Trump has been ridiculed for stating that he will work with them. I will just make one quick point about the current situation. Our last Secretary of State famously pushed the "reset button" during a photo opportunity while in Russia. It was a foolish, childish display of monumental proportions that ignored reality for the sake of a photo opportunity. The Russian leadership probably spilled their vodka that evening while toasting our incompetence. I have great confidence that a Trump administration would not make themselves the fool in this manner.

Trump has built a business empire thinking in terms of lifetimes. His children are now running the business. He has experience planning and acting for the long run. Our corrupt political system has our professional politicians thinking in 2, 4 or 6-year election cycles with very little concern beyond that. The world doesn't work that way. The Chinese and Muslims think and act in terms of centuries. As a businessperson he succeeds by anticipating events rather than constantly reacting to them. He has thought long-term rather than in election cycles. When conditions change, a businessperson changes with them. They don't blindly make decisions based on election promises. Trump has been mocked by the media for not ripping off a list of experienced foreign policy advisers he will rely on if elected. Personally I think we would be better served by unbiased history teachers than the "experts" that have gotten us into this foreign policy mess. Trump would be more likely to keep our finger off the button than on it. And that sounds like a good thing to me.

# The War on Free Speech

"The Framers of the Constitution knew that free speech is the friend of change and revolution, but they also knew that it is always the deadliest enemy of tyranny."

Hugo Black


Trump has unquestionably opened a dialog on issues people are concerned about. Over my lifetime, dialog about serious issues has regressed into arguments about what can be discussed and what cannot. The concept of "political correctness" has suppressed discussion for fear of being called out as an unworthy human being. People shout rather than listen. Trump is unafraid to say what he thinks. He has opened dialog about issues that people feel need to be discussed. Millions of American people are opening their windows and shouting "let's talk about it". It is hard to believe that most people agree with everything Trump says. They just want things openly discussed and resolved for the better. All of our liberties flow from freedom of speech. If speech is repressed, you can bet our liberties will also be repressed. Remember that we are only one Supreme Court Justice away from losing these liberties.

The Federal Government is now pushing "Common Core" on our schools. Make no mistake, this is an effort to teach our children what to believe and what to think. It may be a baby step but it is morphing into the control of our schools by a small group of politicians who will inevitably force their personal ideas and beliefs onto our children. It has happened in totalitarian societies throughout history and it will happen here if left unchecked. It is happening as we speak in our universities.

The public universities are controlled by the government by virtue of the power of the purse. Universities are funded by government subsidies and the availability of student loans guaranteed by the government. Understandably, the administrators owe their allegiance to a bigger, larger government. The government "thought" police are hard at work outlawing the expression of any opinion that disagrees with theirs at our universities. They are supporting various forms of hate speech while outlawing free speech by others. Trump has spoken out against common core.

Political correctness enforced by the "speech" police is truly the path to tyranny. One definition of tyranny is - cruel and oppressive government or rule. Isn't this exactly what happened with Obamacare? Passing this bill was an example of speech repression in its most insidious form. The Speaker of the House of Representatives famously said "we have to pass the bill so that you can find out what is in it, away from the fog of controversy". Replace the words "fog of controversy" with "free speech" and you get the idea.

Obamacare was stuffed down the throats of Americans without one congressional vote by a party representing half of the country's people. It was done in the dark recesses of congress far from the light of day. Opposition was shouted down. People that disagreed with the law were said to be in favor of killing ill people. Details of Obamacare were hidden from the public until after it was passed. Outright lies were told to the public such as "if you like your doctor, you can keep your doctor".

The damage done to Americans has been huge. We have lost our choice of doctor. We have lost our choice of insurance plan. Our money has been appropriated by the government in the form of significantly higher insurance premiums and deductibles. This money is being distributed to special interests chosen by the government. All this happened because a number of professional politicians decided they knew what was best for us. And there was no need for us to talk about it. Just keep quiet and take what we give you.

Climate change is being touted as the biggest threat to humanity in our history. The politicians and special interests are constantly stating that "the science is settled" on global warming. In other words, if you disagree with us just shut up and let us distribute your wealth to the global warming special interests. Personally I don't believe we are even capable of settling the science at this time. Only someone with a God complex would think that they were that smart. I will remind you that in my lifetime we were convinced that global cooling was the problem.

If you are Christian, freedom to express your religious beliefs is being systematically dismantled. All signs of Christianity are being removed from public property. Expressions of a Christian belief in schools is being eliminated. In the interest of brevity, I will use one simple example to illustrate what the speech/thought police are doing. They are trying, and succeeding, in erasing the term "Merry Christmas" from our country. It is now happy holidays or winter break or whatever. It is being stricken from the name of parties, store windows and the lexicon of many media outlets. It is portrayed as discriminatory. Slowly, ever so slowly, it is vanishing like a sun setting over the horizon. It would almost make sense not to recognize one particular religion's holiday if it wasn't so ridiculous in this case. The entire purpose of the holiday is to celebrate the birth of Christ. And a big part of the reason this country exists is because Christians wanted to freely celebrate their faith.

Say goodbye to your football. Think none of the above affects you because you don't care about guns, religion and other such things. Well how would you feel if they took your football away? Stay tuned, it could be coming. The activists are busy working on controlling this part of your life. The linchpin of their efforts is the cause of eliminating concussions. Concussions in sports is a serious issue. Recently a popular movie was released detailing the dangers of concussions. The largest national newspaper also asked the question - is watching football immoral? The people who want to tell you how to think and how to act will stop at nothing until the government has complete control of your life. If you think it can't happen consider the impact these people have had on eliminating school playground activities.

The issue of concussions in football is a perfect example of how far some people will go to eliminate freedom of choice. It is a personal choice made by families and individuals whether or not to participate in football. Our family was faced with a similar decision years ago related to concussions. Our son played a different sport at a high level and had incurred two very serious concussions. We made a decision in which he stopped playing the sport at such a high level for his long-term health. The point is, that it was our decision, not someone's in Washington. It may have been the right or the wrong decision but it was ours. Other people may have made a different decision but it would be their decision.

Politics is rife with people that will shout you down if you express an opinion that differs with yours. They will play the race card or the gender card or any of the cards in their deck. If they don't have an appropriate card, they will just call you mean-spirited or other nasty names. All in an attempt to stifle free expression of thought in order to get what they want. The ends justifying the means. The attitude seems to be that, if the facts don't fit then you must be made to submit. I have never heard Trump seek to divide citizens based on race, residency, gender or any other

characteristic for his own personal gain.
Sometimes he is unkind to the political
elites. Sometimes the truth hurts.

# Returning 10 Million People Back Home

"Hopping the fence or wading the Rio Grande River isn't part of America's immigration process."
Ted Nugent

Regardless of how outrageous it may sound, let's not lose sight of what Trump is saying. He is saying let's return the people who entered our country illegally back to their own country. He goes on to say that they can then apply to re-enter our country legally. Will this happen if Trump is elected President? It is doubtful that 10,000,000+ people will be returned to their own countries. Is the discussion valid? Absolutely. Will criminals be deported and kept out? You can bet on it. As a resident of a border, "invasion state", I certainly hope the criminals are kicked out and kept out. So why is Trump so focused on illegal immigration?

This is, by far, the most difficult campaign issue to write about. It is packed with philosophical, spiritual and moral, almost unanswerable, questions. There are two key core components of the "illegal" immigration question. Who has the right to be inside American borders? Secondly, what do the people "legally" inside the borders owe or want to give to those who decide to enter "illegally". This is not a race issue; it is an illegal vs. legal issue.

The question of who has the right to be on American soil seems pretty clear when viewed in the context of international norms. The citizens of the land encompassed by the boarders of the United States have the recognized right to decide who can enter the country. There may be philosophic questions as to who really owns the land anyway. Aren't we just stewards of the land to be passed on to the next generations? Who was here first? For the most part it doesn't really matter. For purposes of this election it is what it is. To argue against international norms about borders would invite wars and chaos. Trump seems pretty clear on what he believes.

The question of who we want to let in is personal. Like it or not, this country was founded and prospered under a Judeo-Christian value system. These values include love of thy neighbor and helping the less fortunate. As a result, America has been the most charitable country in the history of the world. But this question is not easy to answer without factoring in the economic and societal implications. I choose to believe that most people are good and that Americans want to help as many people as much as they can. Unfortunately, our illegal immigration policies seem to have been driven by politicians and special interests. You can tell who they are since they are the ones shouting "racists" and "bigots" at anyone who would interfere with their votes or interests.

The ability to help others needs to be taken in context. In family terms, our American family is spending more than we make. Significantly more. We are borrowing and spending nearly $1 trillion dollars a year. We are up to our ears in debt. In reality, we have no extra money for anything, we have no savings. We don't even have a single dime saved to pay future Social Security benefits for our own citizens. We can't even afford to supply clean water to the residents of Flint, Michigan. Any incremental money we spend needs to be borrowed. There is always a limit to how much anyone can borrow. There has always been a limit to how long a debtor nation can remain solvent. If a country is not solvent, then its citizens can expect a dramatic reduction in lifestyle. If our entire financial system collapses, we will not be in a position to help anyone.

For years many special interests have tacitly supported illegal immigration in order for big businesses to have a supply of "cheap labor". Others have viewed them as a source of votes. In invasion states, it is not too difficult to vote if you are not a citizen. When you hear a politician say "voting rights" it is code for making it easier for non-citizens to vote. There are also people who want to help those in need. So there are a number of explanations why there are at least 10,000,000 people residing in our country illegally. And these reasons are not mutually exclusive.

Unquestionably, the primary motivation for illegal immigration is economic. Politicians will say - they just want to get a job and work hard at jobs Americans don't want to do in order to support their families. That may be so but it has repercussions for our legal citizens. In areas where illegal immigrants are allowed to work on the cheap, Americans find it harder to get jobs. This was true in my state until a law was passed requiring employers to obtain proof of citizenship in order to hire an employee. There are also those who say - they pay taxes that make up for their cost to our society. Our generous benefits cannot possibly be supported by the low wages earned by the percentage of illegal immigrants that actually do have a tax-paying job. And much of what they take from us is sent back to their native countries.

The cost to citizens of educating and supporting illegal immigrants who live off governmental support is beyond calculation. It undoubtedly costs tens, perhaps hundreds of billions of dollars each year. The aid programs that are available to them range from free health care to food stamps to aid for dependent children to rent subsidies and on and on. In many cases our governments have chosen to allow easy access to these programs, even to non-citizens. The people here illegally know how to access these programs. It is obvious to anyone that uses a hospital emergency room in an invasion state. It would be unreasonable to assume that there wasn't a fair amount of fraud involved as well. As an example, some people claim that they have more children than they actually have, thereby increasing the aid they receive.

If you think all of this doesn't affect you, stay tuned as they move to your state. Ask a person living in an invasion state what is happening in their public schools. Resources are being shifted to educate the millions of illegal immigrants. Class sizes are increasing, electives like art and music are being eliminated, classes for gifted children are being eliminated as resources are poured into English as a second language(ESL). Teaching is being dumbed down so that no one will be left behind.

A big deal was made of Trump's comment on illegals being rapists and murderers. Taken literally it was quite shocking. However only a fool would suggest he meant all of them. How many there are as a percentage of the population is not the issue. But we do know that not an insignificant number are criminals. Probably tens of thousands. We know there are at least thousands of them since Obama proudly released thousands from our prisons to roam freely among American citizens. In the days before political correctness you would have heard about many more of them on the news. Our current administration currently employs a fishing strategy when dealing with illegal immigrant criminals. It's called - catch and release. The only difference is that they ask the released fish to swim back for trial. Want to guess how many come swimming back? So we would guess virtually all of the catch and release criminals are still on the streets of America. Since many are multiple offenders, some do not get released and are over-crowding our prisons.

In any case it is obvious to anyone who wants to see that there are quite a few violent criminals among the illegal immigrants. Many cites have even created safe(sanctuary) zones to protect these criminals from the law. Why would cities have set up all these safe zones if there were no criminals to protect. How many as a percentage of the population is not the issue. You can take it to the bank that most Americans don't want any non-citizen criminals in this country. Only someone with motives contrary to the safety of American citizens would support imported crime. That is Trump's point, he will not tolerate criminals who are not even citizens.

Then there is the question of drug gangs. Anyone can go onto the internet and see videos of heavily armed men running backpacks of drugs around our southern boarders. Illegal immigrants reputedly control large parts of the drug trade in our country. These people are vicious and violent people. We house thousands of them in our prisons at the cost of tens of thousands of dollars a year for each of them. Immigrants in this country legally don't want the criminals either since they are the most likely to be victimized.

It is generally accepted that immigration has been a key factor in our success as a nation. The diversity and energy created by immigrants is undeniable. Closed societies do not fare as well. A modern example is the country of Japan, which is now in a state of decline partially due to their racially closed society. On the other hand, our system of robust and fair laws, along with the enforcement of those laws, has also been important to our nation. No laws, no nation.

Illegal immigration also poses a structural danger to our society. For 200 years the American way of life has prospered under the concept of the melting pot. Peoples of all languages and cultures would assimilate into our society by learning English and adapting our way of life. Most importantly they would take pride in their new country. That has all changed. We have become a decidedly bi-lingual society. Illegal immigrants are almost encouraged to speak their own native language and owe their allegiance to their home country. They can vote, receive benefits, be taught in our schools and get a driver's license, all without knowing a word of English. There are huge areas of invasion cities where not a word of English can be seen. As a result, we have become a politically, socially and economically fractured society. I can't think of a society in the history of the world that has prospered by fostering a fractured society.

The key "right" that can be exercised using Spanish is voting. Logically if people could only vote in English, there would be no incentive for politicians to enable the fracturing of our society. Many politicians also work tirelessly to end any identification procedure for a person to vote. They do this under the guise of not excluding legally entitled citizens of their right to vote. This is obviously not an honest explanation for why they don't want to require identification to be part of the voting process. All citizens have numerous documents to establish their identification. You can't even get on a plane or cash a check without identification as examples. It is widely thought that many people in this country illegally do vote. If this is true, then that could be a key reason many politicians tirelessly encourage illegal immigration.

Until Trump brashly spoke out about illegal immigration we have been blindly traveling down a road to economic and societal destruction. It has become politically incorrect to speak your opinion about illegal immigration if you oppose it. The federal government has decided that they will selectively not enforce immigration laws. Various state and local governments have decided to turn a blind eye to enforcement of criminal laws broken by illegal immigrants. We have been incurring billions upon billions of debt to pay the enormous costs of supporting illegal immigrants. These are death spiral issues that will not resolve themselves. Trump exercised his right of free speech and yanked our heads out of the sand. He is empowering people of all opinions to express their opinions. He clearly states where he stands. He wants to control our boarders. He wants to return people illegally in our country back to their own country. He wants to have people come back to our country legally. He wants to enforce our laws including a zero tolerance policy toward criminal illegal immigrants.

# Can Radical Islamist Terrorism Be Stopped?

"All that is necessary for the triumph of
evil is that good men do nothing"
Edmund Burke


More than 1.5 billion people identify
themselves as Muslims. This amounts to roughly
one out of every four people on earth. They
inhabit virtually every part of the world.
What they believe, I have no idea. My reason
in broaching the subject is the spread of
terrorism by people identifying themselves as
Muslims. Whether you choose to call them
Radical Islamic Terrorists or just plain
terrorists, their actions have the same impact
their victims.

Parts of the world have been under attack
by this form of terrorism for over 1,000
years. Starting in the Middle East and
spreading to southern Europe and India.
Eventually reaching Asia and our own shores.
The brutality they have inflicted on people is
horrendous. I don't believe there is much
dispute in America that it needs to stop.

We had our first battles with them soon
after our country was founded. Muslim pirates
from the north coast of Africa attacked our
merchant ships in order to loot them and

enslave Christians. With hardly a navy to speak of, Thomas Jefferson attacked them in 1801 until they finally decided that messing with us wasn't worth their trouble. Apparently they once again feel it is worthwhile to attack us. It is no wonder, since we send them weapons through their proxy states, while refusing to arm the Kurds and Jordanians that are fighting against them. So what has Trump said we should do?

Trump has talked about cutting off the lifeblood of terrorism, money. He has said we should take their oil which is a primary source of their money. He has also said we should prohibit banks from dealing with terrorists. Cut off their money and you restrict their ability to sustain their activities. He has also said "bomb the hell out of them". Our air-power has almost unlimited ability to thwart their territorial control. It may not appear to be effective but that is only because our current administration has severely restricted our military activities. He has not suggested lots of boots on the ground. A thousand years of history has demonstrated that it just doesn't work. His philosophy appears to be that we should do what we need to do with the least cost and loss of American military lives.

Trump has been criticized for saying he would cut off the terrorists' access to the internet. They have used the internet effectively for recruiting and attack planning. Quite frankly, he doesn't seem to give a darn about their right to free speech if it is used to kill us. He is putting our safety first over political correctness and the special interests of the internet companies.

What Trump has not done is continue the mantra that Islam is a peace loving religion. How would he know if it is? It seems reasonable that he refrains from repeating the mantra if the religious leaders of Islam themselves are not shouting it from the rooftops or aggressively leading the fight against the terrorists.

Trump has also expressed the attitude that our safety is paramount. He has proposed temporarily denying entry into our country for certain Muslims until we can get a handle on the situation. He has also proposed building a wall on the southern border to cut off this avenue of access for terrorists. He is also against the efforts by our current administration to bring in untold thousands of "refugees"(including many military aged men) from the Middle East. He is putting our safety before political correctness. Europe has put political correctness before safety and it is a mess. Rapes of women and terrorist activities are rampant. I have canceled a trip to Paris for that very reason. I like Trump's priorities better than Europe's.

Political correctness has hampered our efforts to stop terrorists by not allowing us to profile them. The following is a personal experience with profiling before political correctness became more important than our safety. When I was 18 I decided to take time off from school after graduating from high school. I looked like a typical hippie. I was young, had long hair and dressed the part, headband and all. Around that time there had been a rash of airplane hijackings. I had a plane change in Chicago during a cross country flight. While waiting for my next plane, I was approached by two suits with badges who asked to speak to me. I accompanied them to a small windowless room where they then proceeded to shake me down. When they were satisfied I was not a threat they turned me loose. I asked them why they had chosen me. They informed me that I fit the profile of a hijacker. I wasn't happy, but neither was I insulted. I didn't want to be hijacked any more than the next guy.

Fast forward to 2002 when my family was inside the Orlando airport. My 9-year-old son was selected to be searched under enhanced security measures due to 9/11. Meanwhile, men of all ages and cultures walked right on through. I remember thinking at the time that we could not be serious if this was our answer to thwarting terrorist attacks. One thing I feel certain about is that Trump will not put political correctness ahead of my safety.

We have experienced dozens of terrorist attacks in our country. Most have been labeled as something else in order to maintain the charade that we are not in danger from Muslim terrorists. The government and media could not cover up the recent murders committed by Muslim terrorists in San Bernardino. At least one neighbor of the terrorists had known something unusual was going on at the terrorists' house. But they had not notified anyone of their suspicions for fear of being called a racist. Political correctness at work! Almost unbelievably, military style equipment, used to respond to just such attacks, was being pulled out of Oakland that very same week. Again, for political correctness reasons. Our current administration has been aggressively removing military style equipment from our cities because they think it just doesn't look politically correct. If you think political correctness can't kill us, think again.

# Let's Make a Deal

"It always seems impossible until its done"
        Nelson Mandela


Conservatives are not happy that Trump has expressed willingness to work with liberals in the congress. Liberals have obviously also not wanted to work with conservatives as they have reelected a president that has demonstrated disdain for anyone that doesn't agree with him. All I can say to them is - get real. There simply aren't that many non-negotiable issues facing our country.

During recent presidential elections, Americans have been virtually evenly split between a "conservative" and a "liberal" candidate. No one side is ever going to get exactly what they want unless it is forced upon the other half that don't agree with them, as was the case with Obamacare. That is not America. Taken to an extreme, it is more like Iraq where the portion of the population in control suppresses the opposition. First under Saddam, and then under the Iranian controlled leaders, different groups have suppressed the others in Iraq. The result has been poverty, and unimaginable bloodshed.

The icon of modern conservatives, Ronald Reagan, was known for his ability to work effectively with members of the opposition party. He acted as if he was president of all Americans, not just those that agreed with him. He spoke in terms of uniting us. He did not denigrate people simply because they had a different view than him. He was reelected in a landslide. His victory demonstrated that we are Americans first, not republicans or democrats. Trump has said unkind things about some of our politicians. I can't say that most of us agree with his approach. But if you listen carefully he does not insult people for what they believe. He attacks them for the way they have acted. That is a big difference if you hope to unite a country.

A strong economy and military make all other things possible. They are non-negotiable. Without these we are simply rearranging the deck chairs on the Titanic. There is more than one way to achieve a strong military and economy. Trump has emphasized both of these pillars of our great nation. He will have his opinions but will negotiate about how to achieve these goals as he has done in business his entire life.

We negotiate continually in our everyday lives. When we negotiate, we are compromising. When we buy a car we negotiate a price that both a seller and a buyer will agree to. Both parties would want a different price but agree to compromise. That is how the world works. Trump has a reputation as a master negotiator. What Trump has said is that he will negotiate good deals with those who disagree with him. I believe that is where conservatives have missed his point.

Conservatives have been angry not because of compromises but rather because there has been little compromise. The professional politicians elected by conservatives have not used their positions to effectively represent their voters. Too often they have simply gotten what they personally needed. They have represented their special interest donors that they need to keep happy in order to get reelected.

The latest budget bill is representative of the "get what I need" mentality. It was passed by funding virtually everything. Significant changes were not made to cut waste or unnecessary spending. Conservatives did not even cut off government support for organizations that harvest baby parts for sale. There was no compromise, it was essentially - let's just spend everything all the politicians need to please their special interest groups. The negotiating was over who got how much. Everyone goes home happy and we continue to spiral into debt. Champaign corks pop all over Washington D.C. and we get the bill. Conservatives may have negotiated but they did not get a good deal for the people who elected them.

This is not just a conservative issue. Millions of liberals have been greatly harmed by the non-negotiated Obamacare law as an example. Liberals have also lost their choice of doctors and seen their medical costs soar as a result of a few people getting what they want with no regard to the majority of Americans. As the medical costs soar for our nation, our economy weakens. Trump would want to negotiate a deal that would provide medical care for all Americans in an effective and efficient manner. Not in a job-killing, economically destructive, manner that causes financial pain for hundreds of millions of Americans.

We have many candidates for president this year. It is important that we judge their ability to effectively make deals and compromises that are in the best interest of the vast majority of Americans. We need someone who has demonstrated the ability to work effectively with people holding different views. Not just domestically but internationally as well. Most of the candidates fall into one of two categories. Worn out professional politicians that have thrived in the currently divisive system or those that have not been effective in bringing about meaningful positive change. Most of them have raised millions from special interest donors. Trump is neither of these. He is a demonstrably successful negotiator. He could not have achieved what he has without the ability to get along with all types of people. He is also self-funding. He cannot be forced into a position by special interest donors.

# Why We Need a Winner Like Trump

"If you don't see yourself as a winner, then you cannot perform as a winner."
Zig Ziglar

When a large company needs a new CEO to run the company, the Board of Directors has the responsibility to make that decision. They based their decision on many factors, not the least of which is relevant prior experience. They evaluate not only what a person has accomplished but also how they accomplished it. They don't give brownie points for how many miles a job candidate has flown or how many meetings they have attended or how many titles they have held. They look for results. When we vote for president, we are hiring a person to lead our country.

They don't ask a candidate to give them a list of all the decisions a new CEO will make over the next four years. Any Board of Directors understands that the world is a very fluid and dynamic environment. The pundits are pounding Trump to give them details of everything he will do. Our country will be better served by a president that will make decisions based on the conditions existing at the time, not based on a canned campaign promise list.

Our country is currently drastically reducing our military capabilities. This is happening with a Democrat president and a Republican congress. Trump has unequivocally stated that he supports a strong military. He has spoken out strongly that our veterans deserve to be treated better and that he would insist that we do so. He has said he will put our safety first in the battle against terrorism and the invasion of illegal immigrants. Trump is also supportive of our police, once again indicating that he puts our safety as a priority.

Trump has stated he will put our economic interests first. He has said he would stop trade deals that ship our jobs to countries like China and Mexico. We spend billions defending South Korea while, as he has stated, buying their TVs due to unfair trade deals. He will stop the spending of billions and billions of dollars to support people that enter our country illegally. Trump is a successful and experienced international businessman. He knows how the system works. He will put our unbelievably talented Wall Street firms to work creating American jobs through sane government policies.

We need a pragmatic cost-conscience person to lead our economy. There are always costs for government actions. A businessperson like Trump has worked under the constraint of only spending what you can afford. We have become a country that is becoming crippled because we spend as much as everyone wants to spend by borrowing. Hundreds of billions of dollars we spend are being wasted or stolen by fraud. Any of dozens of American companies could rapidly design systems to eliminate waste and fraud in programs such as Medicare and Obamacare if we cared to do it.

Trump will have no incentive to strip away our rights and freedoms. Behind every freedom we lose are professional politicians and special interests with something to gain. Votes and money flow from dividing us. By self-funding his campaign, he will owe no favors to those that wish to strip away our freedoms. Although he says some unkind things about politicians and the media, Trump does not campaign by attempting to divide our citizens.

What is happening in our inner cities is a disgrace. Millions of people are living in crime-infested, burned out neighborhoods with not a job in sight. The very politicians claiming to represent them have created an inequality of life in addition to an inequality of income. All the while, the professional politicians that claim to represent them waste money that could be used to help them. They hang out with Hollywood celebrities, take luxurious family trips around the world and play golf. Trump isn't running for president to do these things. He can do that now with his own money. He is running to work hard to improve the lives of all Americans.

America loves a winner. Trump is a winner with a big personality and a bigger presence. He has not been run over by the media or the politicians that try to shout him down or to smear him. If elected, he will have the tenacity and winning persona to accomplish much of what he has said he will do. He will also provide inspiration to other politicians that have been afraid to buck the system. He has the potential to help elect a new breed of office holder that will actually do the will of the people.

This election may be the last chance to avoid irreparable damage to our future. The greatest imminent danger is the voting control by politicians that benefit from people paid not to work. These politicians have been busy getting more and more people dependent on government aid programs. They have greatly expanded the voter base that have no option but to vote for someone who continues to keep the work-free lifestyle as part of government policy. They are establishing a permanent underclass voter base of non-English speaking immigrants (legal and illegal). We are rapidly approaching the point where people who live off the government outnumber those who don't. We also have a rapidly weakening job market and economy We are incurring an ever increasing national debt. And our military is being systematically dismantled, putting us in harm's way from those who wish us ill.

If you like the mess we are in, you have plenty of professional politician candidates to choose from. You even have two members of political Royal families to vote for. You even have a socialist if the mess isn't expanding fast enough for you. They know how to spend your money. Most of them have more baggage than a porter on the Orient Express.

If you want at least a shot at righting our sinking ship, Trump is your man.

About the Author:

Ken Julien is a retired business executive turned author. He is a CPA and MBA. Born into a working class family he has been a member of six unions including the UAW. Ken resides in Arizona.

## Copyright

www.ingramcontent.com/pod-product-compliance
Lightning Source LLC
Chambersburg PA
CBHW072144280526
45788CB00002B/776